DATING Dares

Dating Prep
Published by Casting Seeds Publishing

Scripture quotations unless otherwise indicated are from the ESV ® Bible (The Holy Bible, English Standard Version), Copyright © 2001 by Crossway. Used by permission. All rights reserved.

Copyright © 2018 by Joshua Eze
Cover design by Jacob Morgan | jacobbmorgan.dribbble.com/

All Rights Reserved. No Part of this book may be reproduced or transmitted in any form or by any means, electronic or mechanical, including photocopying and recording, or by any information storage and retrieval system, without permission in writing from the publisher.

Published in the United States by Casting Seeds Publishing an extension and aid to UNPLUGGED.

***

Websites and Social Media sites:
Website: IAMUNPLUGGED.COM | MYCOACHJOSH.COM
Social Media: **@MYCOACHJOSH**

Table of Contents

Intro |How to read and how to play | 9
My two and a half cents | 11
You are never alone | 43
Wholeness | 45
Self-Awareness | 48
Access Levels | 50
Before you Date | 56
Four Stages of Growth | 65
Pure motives | 67
For those that are Married | 70
Family Tree Questions | 71
Family Traditions | 74
Family Attributes | 76
Significant Memories | 77
Our Family Tree | 78
Children | 80
Church Hurt | 81
Family Support Systems | 83
$$$ | 88
Location, Location, Location | 90
Communicating Concerns | 90
Pet Peeves | 94
A Marriage of Legacy | 96
Do you have any concerns? | 97
Feeling Rushed? | 98
Noticing Anything? |99
Love Languages | 100
Views on Sex | 101
Are we Rooted? | 102
Habits and Hobbies Questions | 107
Celebrating Accomplishments | 109
Emotional Reactions | 110
Fun Favorites | 111
More Moment more Problems Solved | 113
Deal Breakers | 114
Do I annoy You? | 115
The Good and The Bad | 116
Sexual Habits | 116
Addictions | 117
Godly Habits | 119

When are date nights? | 121
Did you play Sports? | 123
Are you stressed? | 124
Health | 125
THEO Questions | 129
What do you believe in Spiritually? | 129
Is Jesus God? | 130
How are you and God? | 132
Church Hurt | 133
Prayer | 135
The Bible | 139
Has God confirmed it? | 144
Sex and Temptations | 148
Spiritual Warfare | 151
Wrestling with God | 152
Past, Present and Possibilities Questions | 157
Past Relationships | 159
Do you want Children | 159
Credit Score | 160
Anger Management | 160
Do you have a STD? | 162
What are your intentions with me? | 163
Ex's | 163
$$$ | 164
Can you handle your wife making more than you? | 165
Passions and goals | 166
Time Management | 169
Your Accountability | 172
Prayer List | 175
What do you want in a spouse? | 176
Where do you see us in 5 to 10 years | 177
Your Favs Questions | 179
Extras!
1 Year Relationship Tracker | 184
1 Year Off-Season Singleness Tracker | 233
Wins and Lessons | 259
How to handle a break up | 260
Winning and Learning | 261
What to consider before leveling up | 262

Dating Prep

Welcome to The Dating Prep book. This book was designed to help you prep for your date nights whether before you get into a relationship or marriage or while you are in one. The pointers and resources in this book will help you discern deeper your potential candidate or to develop and deepen the connection you already have in your marriage. Five categories make up this book and the game. The categories are;

1. Family Tree
2. Habits and Hobbies
3. Your Favs
4. Theo
5. Past Present and Potential

These categories make up the different areas of a person's life. Each of these is self-explanatory the only one that you may be wondering about is THEO. THEO is short for Theology. Each category will have a list of questions and explanations that are separated into stages. There are three stages, and they are;

1. **Cloud**: Beginning stages of the relationship
2. **Cement**: When reality sets in
3. **Corporation**: Time to go to the next level or to build your marriage.

FLAGS

Each stage is important, and certain questions should be asked at each stage to help you better discern your potential prospect or to understand your husband or wife better. There are also four flags to be mindful of, and they are;

1. Red – Whoa
2. Yellow – Slow
3. Green – Go
4. White – No

Feel free to utilize these flags to respond to how your potential prospect or wife/husband answer your questions.

Wins and Lessons + Winning and Learning

This book was also designed to be a workbook for you to track your relationship whether alone or with your significant other. There are areas for you to reflect on yourself as well as write down their answers. There are also activities to help you guys bond as a couple. At the end of the book are two sections; these sections are designed to help you journal your relationship experiences. One section is called Wins and Lessons, and the other one is called Winning and Learning. Wins and lessons is for if you and the person you are with break up you can utilize this area to write down what you learned from the relationship etc. Winning and Learning is for when you guys have levelled up to engagement or marriage, and they have received the God-Certified stamp of approval. You can utilize this section to write down what you are learning, and the wins you guys have acquired together.

Help me help more relationships.

If you love the Dating Prep materials and know friends or family members that could benefit from these materials do me a big favor and spread the word by either sharing on your social media platforms or just simply sharing your experience with a close friend or family member. I really want to create resources that will help decrease the divorce rate in our world. I believe the right questions at the right stage could really help save a lot of people from either starting a bad relationship or help save a marriage from a divorce. Thank you again for all your support. Have Fun!

Hashtags to use: #datingprep #mydatenightgame #mycoachjosh #joshuaeze + Feel free to tag me I would love to see your pictures and comments! Much Love – Coach

Do you relate to you? (Self-examination)

What I mean by the question above is; are you in tune with yourself? Are you composed, still, maturing, focused, balanced, whole and connected to God? So many of us are all over the place on the inside. Bad thoughts are trespassing in our minds and our emotions are boiling over. We are confused, unstable and easily swayed. Some of us are sailing alone without a captain, and we wonder why we sink only meters from the shore. Before we endeavor to sail the married seas, we must have conversations on the dock. We must talk with God and sit with him for years on the shore allowing him to develop us and prepare us so that when it's time to sail we will have him, a matured us and a person selected by him to join us. Before we can leave the harbor, we have to let go of every hurt, offence or resentment that we are harboring in our hearts. Your relation-ship will determine the places you will go and the baggage that you bring on it will be what the enemy uses to sink that ship. It's crazy how many injured people are trying to play in the game called love again? Love is a rough sport and a lot of immature people are playing in this league, and you must be careful and be like Kawhi Leonard from the Spurs and hold out so that you can receive your max deal. Injuries happen, but you have to allow them to heal so you won't poke holes in the relationship causing it to sink. To relate to your purpose and who you were created to be, you must relate to God. No one deserves to be entangled in your dysfunctions; find God, function properly and then let him fit you with the one he has for you.

You must relate to your purpose before you can relate to someone else. If you don't know who you are, and what you are supposed to do, how will you be able to know who is for you. So many people are selecting based on the moments but not based on a mission. A person who has a mission will select accordingly to the mission. Who are you? What are you supposed to do? What kind of person do you truly want? What do you want your marriage now to be known for? It all boils down to knowing the you He ↑ Knows. Imagine where your singleness, relationship or marriage could be if you improved daily even if it's half a percent a day? Imagine the impact you and your family could have if you always endeavored to grow and evolve? No matter how smart you are or how attractive you are; smarts and attraction fades. You are the sum of your character period, and you have to make sure you define the character you are going to play in this movie called life. It is your choice. Before you can relate to someone else, you must relate to God and to you.

Do you relate to others? (Supporters)

All of us need support, but not everyone can support us. We may all be in the same book but not all of us are on the same page and even if we are on the same page not all of us are on the same sentence or word on that page. Pace, peace, preparation, placement, progression, patience, purpose, passion and perspective all play a part in who we should be supported by and who we can support. Not everyone should be connected deeply to us due to the different ideas and perspectives we share. Let's look at these Ps.

Pace:

Pace matters. So many people are pursuing things at the wrong pace. Pursuing things too slowly or too fast can lead to the missing of or the mismanagement of opportunities. When it comes to a mate, you must observe their work ethic because if you're a go-getter type of person, but they are lazy, there will be conflicts. On the other hand, if you are one that discerns before diving, but they are dangerous and reckless then that will cause conflicts as well. For a relationship or a marriage to thrive, there must be a steady pace that is birth out of peace. With God, there is no rush. Everything is set already and established; all we are required to do is to obey. Easier said than done but it is important. Image if you mastered obedience; imagine the opportunities and the open doors you would have right now? Pace matters and linking up with someone that understands your stride is vital to the marriages overall success. You do not want to be with someone or be someone that is not paced. Now don't get me wrong you need to be with someone that can push and pull you. Push you to the right pace or pull you or slow you down to the right pace but overall the pace must be set by God, and when the both of you relate with him you will be able to discern the pace he wants the both of you to be at.

Singles:

What are three things you are pursuing right now and →	How is your pace at pursuing them? Too slow – slow – perfect pace – fast or too fast
1	
2	
3	
How could your current pace at pursuing these things affect your future relationship?	
Where in your life right now do you need to trust God more, helping you to find his pace for you?	

Dating/ Married Individuals:

When it comes to pursuing goals what kind of person are you and what kind of person are they?	
You:	Them:

Do you guys complement or contradict each other's pace? In what ways?	

What are three things you are pursuing right now and how are they complementing or contradicting their pace?	
1	How:
2	How:
3	How:

What are three things they are pursuing right now and how are you complementing or contradicting your pace?	
1	How:
2	How:
3	How:

What is God's pace for you both and what are some ways to ensure you both maintain his pace?

Peace:

There is nothing like peace. Peace may be one of the top if not the top thing people are searching for. Many people take drugs; form habits, select friends and spouses trying to search for it but cannot find true peace. There is a difference though between our temporal peace and Gods eternal peace. Many people are looking for a peace that **matches** their understanding versus the one that **surpasses** it. God's peace is a peace that will surpass your understanding; it may not change it immediately, but it is tangible proof that he heard you and that he is involved. We need people who carry this kind of peace. Imagine being with someone who carries more problems than they do peace. Imagine the mixed climate that will be in your home. You want to make sure you are supported by peacemakers not peace takers. You also must make sure that you are a peaceful support for your spouse or your potential one. Do you instigate problems, are you a worrier or are you a person that calms the restlessness in others?

Everyone:

Are you at peace? Why or why not?

What is affecting your peace?

List below all of the places you visit and all of the people that you engage with most and beside each one write whether you are a peace taker or a peacemaker.

Places and Names	Peace taker or Peacemaker?

What problems are you carrying right now that could rob the peace of a potential mate or your current mate and what must you do to allow God's peace to turn you into a peacemaker?

Preparation:

They say that success happens when preparation meets opportunities. So many people have missed opportunities due to them not being prepared. The same goes for our relationships. Our current relationships are a reflection of our preparation. The lack of preparation is the reason why many marriages fail. Your singleness is or was a season given to you by God to prepare for your purpose and your potential mate. The lack of preparation will lead to unnecessary issues that will by default sink your relationship. There are just certain things that cannot go into a marriage, and they are lust, anger, pride, selfishness, ego, jealousy, discontentment, constant worrying, baggage etc. you have to assess your life before you grant access to it and you have to thoroughly assess a potential mates life before you grant them access to you. Not everyone deserves access to you; they have to be prepared to cherish, guard and engage your worth. The sad thing though is, many people don't know their worth and due to their ignorance, they allow unqualified, ill-equipped individuals into their lives that sabotage their souls leaving it with deep wounds. I'm sure there are many married people now who can attest they wished they knew their worth before getting married to the person they are married to. For those that are married to a genuine person, preparation can sustain you both during the next storm.

Life is a cycle of good times, bad times, indifferent times and trying times and your preparation now could help your wife as she approaches motherhood your husband as he loses his mother. We all must make sure that we are prepared not just in our physical ability but in our mental, emotional and spiritual abilities as well. So many people are unequally yoked. There may be an equal yoke in attraction, but there is no equal yoke when it comes to the things of God. Imagine being yoked up with a person that cannot pray or is too hard-hearted to empathize with you or is not mentally renewed enough to understand what you need now. Waiting on Gods perfect timing is so important. So many people are restless with this truth to the point that they settle outside of it and wonder why they are yoked up with a person that cannot sustain them. Any relationship that was conceived outside of God's perfect timing or is without God completely will naturally have damaging effects in them. Resistance should only come from outside of the relationship not from within and most resistances that are within relationships is due to a lack of preparation.

Everyone:

List below all of the character traits you would like to see in your future or current marriage and beside them write either prepared to offer or not prepared to offer.

Character Traits	Prepared or not prepared
1	
2	
3	
4	
5	
6	
7	
8	

What must you do now to prepare to offer what you would like to see in your marriage?

Singles/ Dating

List below all of the traits you would like in a potential mate and beside each trait write, whether you match or do not match these traits. This exercise is for traits not talents. You are not going to always match a person's talent but you should both match in character traits like faithfulness, kindness, love etc.

Traits and Lifestyle	Match or don't match
1	
2	
3	
4	
5	
6	
7	
8	
9	
10	
11	

12	
13	
14	
15	
16	
17	
18	
19	
20	
How many traits do you match or don't match →	Match #	Don't match #
What must you do to improve in the areas you do not match?		

Married Individuals:

What does your significant other desire to be in their life (mother, father, business owner, etc.) and how prepared are you to support them in those areas?

Their desires	Prepared or not prepared
1	
2	
3	
4	
5	
6	
7	
How many areas are you prepared or not prepared for? →	Prepared #	Not prepared #

What must you do to prepare your heart to serve them in the areas you answered not prepared?

Placement is like preparation. So many people are performing well out of place. Performing well in the wrong place gets you no points in heaven. Some preachers were supposed to be engineers, some engineers were supposed to be missionaries; some missionaries were supposed to be doctors and so on and so on. They're probably making a lot of money but are not producing in the places where God wants them to produce. Placement is important. Knowing your place goes far deeper than a profession, it also represents gender roles. When a man knows his sacrificial place and his wife knows, her submissive place, and they both together know their place in God then their marriage will thrive. It is our responsibility as believers to know what the word of God says about our roles. A sacrificial man is a man that sees the needs of his family and sacrifices his selfish desires for the betterment of the family. In too many situations, men are selfish and are not willing to sacrifice their boyhood dreams for their family but instead sacrifice their family to see those dreams come to past. Like I always tell men; finish the assignments of your single years before you pursue a woman because if you do not, you will try to start a marriage while trying to finish those assignments at the same time setting yourself up for failure. God will bring you your wife when he sees that it is not good for you to be alone anymore and the one God has for you will be able to help you fulfil your dreams and vice versa. The same goes for women; a lot of women either do not know how to be submissive to a good man or are being submissive to the wrong one. The beautiful thing about women is that they get to choose whom they submit to. Do not allow insecurities or loneliness to cause you to give wife-like benefits to a boyfriend. Why would a man show you the respect you deserve or move the relationship forward if he is already receiving marriage-like treatment before marriage? A woman of standards will weed out the bad because she will reserve her goods for a man that will pursue her for her and not just for her goods.

Everyone: Profession

Where does God want you right now?

If you do not know where he wants you what must you do to find out... and how could not knowing your place affect your future or current relationship?

Everyone: Know your role!

What does the word of God say about your role as a man or a woman in a relationship or marriage? Search and write down below scriptures that talk specifically about your role as a man, woman, husband or wife and beside each one check off if you match what that scripture says. In the last box write down areas you need to improve!

Scriptures	What does it say about your role	Check

In what areas do you need to improve?

Progression

One of the worst places to be in is in a relationship with a person that refuses to grow. Do not marry potential marry **progression**. So many people are distracted by a person's potential and are not focused on that person's work ethic. A person cannot reach their full potential without a steady progression. We all need running mates to help encourage us down the road. We need people that can keep up the pace and motivate us to continue forward. We need people who are not just starters but finishers. People who can see beyond your pain and see the potential behind it. So many people settle for people who have great potential - they are smart, athletic and gifted but either lack faith in themselves or a solid work ethic. You want to yoke yourself up with a person that is self-medicated and self-motivated; people who can function without burning someone else out. They know how to medicate themselves through the word of God, and they know how to motivate themselves in the presence of God. Potential is nothing but a dream. Don't put your stock in a person's potential instead put your stock in a person's progression. The glory of God is key. The placement of a person's glory will determine the quality of their grind. A person who solely wants God to be glorified will grind with you, for you but never over you or through you. So many people are fueled by carnal glory and success that they will run over their families to get it. Progression without the proper pursuit of God's glory will destroy anything in its way. A healthy marriage or relationship is with a person whose grind is for Gods glory because when that person grinds for God, God will be in control of that person's gears controlling their pace. You need a person who honors the conviction of the Holy Spirit and who allows him to control their pace. Not all progression is a good progression.

Everyone:

What is your potential?

What kind of work ethic do you have towards your potential? Write below either strong, steady, so, so, suspect or stagnant and write your reasons why?

Work-ethic: →	Stagnant	Suspect	So-so	Steady	Strong
Why:					

Dating

What is your prospects potential?					
How is their work ethic? →	Strong	Steady	So-so	Suspect	stagnant
Is it worth pursuing the relationship why or why not?					

Married:

What is your husbands or wife's potential?					
How is their work ethic? →	Strong	Steady	So-so	Suspect	stagnant
In what ways could you help them tap into it?					

Patience:

Not everyone is graced with the patience for you, and that is ok. God has dealt to every person a measure of faith or function, and not everyone can handle the weight that comes with each person's function or faith. Everyone has a scope given to them by God some people have a;

- **Home scope** where their purpose is to tend the home and focus solely on raising their children and helping their spouse fulfil their God-given purpose.
- **Neighborhood scope**: where their purpose is to influence and serve their local community both around where they live and around their local church, making disciples building their local body etc.
- **City Scope**: where their purpose is to serve various communities in their city; helping solve the issues that have become a stain on their city.
- **State Scope**: where they serve multiple cities in their state helping the state at large progress.
- **Regional and National Scope**: where they serve their region or their nation helping advance the causes of God regionally and nationally.
- **Global Scope**: where they travel country-to-country planting churches, establishing businesses and resources helping people from all over find God and the solutions to their problems.

Knowing a person's scope is important because if you have been dealt a neighborhood measure but marry a person with a global measure then there may be conflicts in the home. Now that does not mean two different measures can't come together, but there must be a grace there to support each other. It's hard to have grace in an area where you lack experience or revelation and empowerment from God. Some people grew up in a home where the dad or mom had a global scope but they as an individual were called to a house scope. The son or daughter that grew up in this home would be familiar with what a global scope person would need and through experience and the gift of grace given to them by God will be able to support a person with a global scope.

It is ok to be honest and know what you are able to handle. A person who knows their purpose and their measure will allow God to connect them because they know whomever God connects them with will be able to handle their scope. The glue that keeps relationships together is God. If God did not conceive it or is allowed in it, then that relationship or partnership will fail. Patience is a gift from God. For patience to have her perfect work in any of our lives, we must have revelation or understanding. It's easier for me to wait when I understand why I am waiting, it's easy for me to walk with someone through a tough time when I know that they were placed there by God. It's easier for me to serve and operate in my calling if I know why and understand the ways of God. Impatience's is birthed when we choose not to humble ourselves under God's explanation and purpose for things and situations. When we know God is in control and trust his Character and timing, then we can wait patiently knowing that he loves us and is leading us down a path of preparation and purpose. Grace and patience are important; without it relationships die but when God is in the mix and his purpose and character is understood and accepted then he will supply both people with the grace they will need to handle each other's unique scopes.

Purpose:

Everything under the **Son** has a purpose. You have a purpose, I have a purpose your marriage has a purpose, your business has a purpose your ministry has a purpose. Everything connected to you and everything that is channeled through you has a purpose. A person without a sense of purpose always settle, but a person on purpose does everything with a purpose. Purpose kind of goes with the scope points I talked about earlier. You want to make sure you are with a person that shares the same goals and desired outcomes as you. That does not mean you have to love and support the same groups of people or industries it just means you guys share the same heart for God and for those you are to reach. It can get tricky though, and you have to be clear in your singleness so you will be able to discern the will of God. So many people silence their purpose out of their need for companionship. They will forfeit their dream to be with someone and will serve their dream while letting theirs die. God knows how to connect you with a spouse or to deepen your connection with yours and make it a relationship of purpose. Purpose is important and knowing yours early will cause you to pace yourself before pursuing a relationship with another person.

Everyone:

Would you consider yourself a patient person?	Y or N
Why or why not	
What do you not have patience for and why?	
1	Why:
2	Why:
3	Why:
4	Why:
5	Why:
6	Why:
7	Why:
In what ways is God testing your patience?	Why is patience important in a relationship?

Scope:

What is your scope →	
What is their scope →	

Not Married Yet: Honestly; can you guys make it work →	Yes or No
How can it work? How can it not work?	

Married: How can you make it work?

Passion:

Passion is the fuel of purpose. If you want to find your purpose find your passion. Your passion is what you want to see changed in the world it's your guide to the proximity of who you were created to be and what you were created for. Passions must match in a relationship not necessary as I said before for the same people group or industry but there must first be the same height in flame as far as a passion for God.

Being in a relationship or marriage with a person that does not match or inspire your passion for God will cause your relationship to be lopsided or stagnant. It is important for couples to develop habits that will ensure their fire for God will continue to burn in their relationship. So many of us are periodically passionate for God but are not permanently passionate. For some of us, we add logs to our love for God only once a week, once a month, once a quarter or even once a year. Many of us do not have a daily regiment to keep the flame of God kindled. The best way for Satan to keep us periodically passionate or not at all is to cause us to be either overly busy or preoccupied with cares. We must fight for our place in faith. We must fight for our place of consistency and live our lives from a place of being fully persuaded not partially persuaded. Imagine what a couple could do with high levels of passion for God causing them to be balanced in their passions for each other, their craft etc.? When a couple continuously seeks God and his will for them and implements and engages in regiments that keeps their passion for Him ablaze they will begin to do exploits. Our passion for God balances out our external passions. You do not want to be with someone who is more passionate about you or their purpose more than they are about God.

God requires us to love in this order:

1. Him (God)
2. Yourself
3. Your Significant other/ family
4. Ministry, career, purpose, other people

Let me explain what a balanced love is. A balanced love is a love that does not lure you into sin or into deep, dark emotions. It's a love that sees deeper into the needs of God, yourself and others and allows you to move peaceably and cautiously. Love is for the mature. Most people are in lust not in love. The definition of love can be found in 1st Corinthian's. 13:4-8 Love is patient and kind; love does not envy or boast; it is not arrogant or rude. It does not insist on its way; it is not irritable or resentful; it does not rejoice at wrongdoing but rejoices with the truth. Love bears all things, believes all things, hopes all things, endures all things. Love never ends. Lust's definition is found in 1st Corruptions 13:4-8 Lust is impatient and selfish, lust envy's and boast, it is arrogant and rude. It insists on its way, it is irritable and produces resentment; it rejoices at wrongdoing and ignores the truth. It burdens all things, deceives all things, hinders all things, and erodes all things. Lust ends things.

Love is balanced. Anytime you find yourself at one of two extremes you are in lust or some form of carnal desire and it is important to be in a relationship with a person that is pursuing God passionately and is endeavoring to have a balanced love with God, themselves, you and their purpose.

Everyone:

Your flame for God is →	Out	Smokey	Warm	Hot	Ablaze
Their flame for God is →	Out	Smokey	Warm	Hot	Ablaze
What compromises in your life are affecting your flame?		What compromises in their life are affecting their flame?			
What do you need to do to increase your flame?		What do they need to do to increase their flame?			

Perspective

How you see things and how your significant other see things are important. God cares more about how you guys see things than just your ability to see them. He cares about how you see

- Him
- Life
- Marriage
- Sex
- Money
- The opposite sex
- Yourself
- Time
- Community
- Accountability
- Your calling
- Others
- Family
- Children

And so on and so on. He cares because how we see these things will determine how we function in and with these things. God cares about our ability to manage things, and our management ability is predicated on our perspectives. Not everyone shares the same perspectives. Some people do not think it's right to reprimand kids some do. Some people don't see it as important to save money or are not aggressive in learning money management some do. It is important to observe and analyze how people see these things because if you see them correctly, and they don't see them correctly or if they see them correctly, but you don't it will cause an unbalance in the relationship. Only the creator has the clearest perspective on his creation. All of the things listed above are found in God. Your level of relationship with God will determine how you see His intent for these things to be used and enjoyed. How do you see the items listed above and have you taken the time to find out God's view on them? Trust me it is better to understand these things and to incorporate habits to sustain them during your single years than to try to find them or have to deal with a spouse that is blind to them.

Everyone: Beside each perspective, I want you to write either poorly or properly in your column and in the column of your significant other. If you are single just write under your column. In the last column, write scriptures that pertains to each area symbolizing how God wants you to see it. In the bottom box write out what you will need to do to improve in the areas you have a poor perspective.

Perspectives	How do you see	How do they see	How does God want you to see
Him			
Life			
Marriage			
Sex			
Money			
The opposite sex			
Yourself			
Time			
Community			
Accountability			
Calling			
Others			
Family			
Children			
Improvements:			

Each of these P's are important to observe before you get into a relationship and are important in growing the one you are currently in.

***

If you are in a relationship with a person and you are not sure if it is of God, you need to really slow the relationship down and seek God immediately. Stop all forms of intimacy and take it slow because you don't want to waste your time or theirs. If you are married to a person, and you feel drained and don't feel like they are helping you or are helping themselves then you need to do the following;

First, increase your time in developing your relationship with God and rejuvenate yourself because it's hard to fight the warfare against your marriage drained. You need to find a quiet place in your home, car or office to build yourself up in your most holy faith. You need to start patching up your wounds and renewing your mind so that you will stop looking on your spouse as your enemy but the enemy working through your spouse. During this phase, you will need to incorporate habits that will build you up. You will need to develop a worship, and praise playlist on Spotify, Apple Music or Google play and set out time to strictly worship God and welcome his presence into your life to help you heal. Next, go to openbible.info and type under the topical section the areas you need help in for instance if you feel weary then type in scriptures on weariness and meditate on those scriptures with a notebook and journaling your experience with them. As I always say before you work with any of these resources make sure you personally from your heart welcome the Holy Spirit to join you and to lead you, and watch how he supernaturally helps you over time.

Secondly, you need to plan your attack against the demonic entities working against your marriage. You are going to need to observe the demonic character traits that are evident in your relationship. If its defiance pray against defiance if its bitterness fight against that spirit of un-forgiveness or bitterness. Do whatever it takes to not fight your spouse but to fight against the enemy working in and through your spouse. Constantly utilize the prayer below when you feel the pressure come against you when you do this because they will pressure you. As I always tell people, resistance is proof your prayers are working. Many people stop at the moment they feel resistance from their spouse and stop praying causing the satanic cord to wrap around their spouse tighter and tighter. That's why it's important to continuously build your faith during this process and know that they are not upset with you it's just the demons in them are causing them to be upset and irritable.

Prayer: Father God in the name of Jesus I thank you for your purpose in my life and my marriage. I thank you that you are with us even if we are not at the moment with each other. Father God I repent of all bitterness and un-forgiveness in my heart towards _____

And I confess my personal sins of

_____
_____
_____

and I thank you father God that you are faithful to your word in forgiving me and setting me free from all personal sins and resentments that will hinder the effects of this prayer. I thank you God, and I love you. Now in the name of Jesus, I come against every demonic spirit of (Name the character traits in your spouse or around your marriage), _____,
_____, _____,
_____, _____.

and I come against every spell, hex, or any work of the demonic including witches, warlocks and any individual knowing or unknowing working against my marriage. I cancel your plots and schemes now in the name of Jesus. Leave my marriage and my life now in the name of Jesus. Amen

Once you have said this prayer, I want you to get a little bottle with a top and fill it up with olive oil, and I want you to pray this prayer over it say → Father in the name of Jesus I set this bottle of oil aside for your use. This bottle of oil is holy unto you, and everything it touches is touched with the healing and delivering work of Jesus. The power is not in the oil but in the power it represents so I Heavenly Father I believe by faith that this bottle will do your work in Jesus name.

Once you have done that I want you to place a cross with that oil on every doorpost of your home and say → in the name of Jesus, I sanctify this post and rebuke every demonic spirit from entering or terrorizing my home.

After you have anointed the door post, I want you to anoint yourself as often as you see fit and say → I am covered under the protection of my lord and savior Jesus Christ and if you want you can while your husband, wife or children are sleep anoint them with oil and pray over them as well. This is important because you have authority in Christ to save your home.

Once you have done these three things I want you to simply be kind, loving, patient, gracious, gentle and humble. War in private love in public.

Healing Habits Accountability Checklist: Loving the Hell of your home!
What demonic/ carnal character traits are evident in your home?
1
2
3
4
5
6
7
Strategic Love: in what ways can you be more kind, loving, patient, gracious, gentle and humble with them? - What are their favorite things to do, eat, drink, etc.:

Worship: write down below the platform you created your playlist on, the date you created the playlist and the number of songs on your list.

Platform:	Date:	# of songs:

Scriptures: What issues are you struggling with in your marriage and what scriptures did you find on openbible.info to support your issue?

Struggles:	Scriptures:
1	
2	
3	

4	
5	

Build your faith checklist: Write down below the days and times you plan to worship, pray and read scriptures and utilize the weekly checklist below to hold you accountable.

What days and times will you spend doing the following:							
Worship →	Days:			Time:			
Meditate on Scriptures	Days:			Time:			
Time in Prayer →	Days:			Time:			
WK#1	Mon	Tues	Wed	Thurs	Fri	Sat	Sun
Worship							
Scriptures							
Prayer							
In what ways did you feel your faith increase this week:		Any improvements in your spouse?			Areas for you to improve this week?		
WK#2	Mon	Tues	Wed	Thurs	Fri	Sat	Sun
Worship							
Scriptures							
Prayer							
In what ways did you feel your faith increase this week:		Any improvements in your spouse?			Areas for you to improve this week?		

WK#3	Mon	Tues	Wed	Thurs	Fri	Sat	Sun
Worship							
Scriptures							
Prayer							
In what ways did you feel your faith increase this week:		Any improvements in your spouse?				Areas for you to improve this week?	

WK#4	Mon	Tues	Wed	Thurs	Fri	Sat	Sun
Worship							
Scriptures							
Prayer							
In what ways did you feel your faith increase this week:		Any improvements in your spouse?				Areas for you to improve this week?	

***

You are never alone

(Laziness, loneliness, longing, lingering, latching, and losing)

The conception of a lot of unbalanced and unequal relationships/ marriages is loneliness. Loneliness is a state of mind it is a perspective that derives from idolatry and false expectations. Many people have idolized the idea of marriage with no intent of preparing for it. They want love but are not ready to be in love. Their false expectations for love has either caused them to remain single or to be in and out of relationships. A person with false expectations will either cause a burden to another person causing them to leave them or will shun away prospects due to unrealistic demands. Loneliness too can become a state of mind in a believer's heart due to them being impatient with God. Many believers have a hard time dealing with God's timing and that is understandable because I too struggled at one point, but when I adopted the right perspective of Gods timing and witnessed the rewards of his timing, I began to say God however long. People with the wrong perspective of God's character and timing will always scream God How long, but those who understand the will of God and know how to deal with their frustrations are quick to say God however long.

The bible says that they that wait on the Lord shall renew their strength they will mount up with wings like eagles, they will run and not grow weary they will walk and not faint. The key word in this verse is **wait**. The word wait here does not mean to sit and do nothing it means to serve like a waiter or a waitress. When we serve God, our strength is renewed helping us to mount, run and walk without burnout. We lose energy when we serve ourselves, others and our purpose but not God. For me to have the energy for my needs, the needs of others and for my purpose, I must serve God. God is the only one that can truly sustain you in whatever phase you are in. If you are not serving God single how are you going to be able to know how to serve your future spouse with peace, joy, patience, kindness, and love? If you are not serving, God married how are you going to be able to know how to lift up and strengthen your spouse. His strength is made perfect in our weakness. None of us can be kind, loving, patient, gentle, without God. We have to acknowledge to God that we are weak and unable to do anything without him and allow him to strengthen us with power and perspective to function properly but none of this is possible with a mind that is **lonely**. You are never alone. Even if you feel alone in your marriage, you are not alone. Your greatest resource is not your husband or wife or your money etc. it is God. When you know that he is a present help in the time of trouble and that he is near the brokenhearted and that he is one whisper away from all the wisdom you need you will be strengthened in times when tempted to adopt a lonely mindset. My greatest time is my alone time with God. His presence is the #1 presence I seek because seeking his presence and becoming familiar with it will teach me how to be present in the various areas of my life. But when I choose to be idle, I will idolize the idea of any, and everything I feel will give me value.

The key to success on earth is servant hood. My service to God will permeate how I serve myself, how I serve others and how I serve my purpose. Laziness, the opposite of service, fuels the mindset of loneliness. It is hard to dwell on loneliness when being productive in your purpose. Those that are lazy have lost sight of their assignments and have opened the door for idle/ idol thoughts to creep into their minds. See, Satan has a plan for lazy people; he knows that lazy people or people who are spiritually lazy will by default feel ill-equipped to function at their current stage of life. They will feel that God is not helping them or is taking too long. These trails of thoughts will then develop a mindset that feels alone or feels that they cannot connect to God and this new mindset of loneliness will then lead to **longing**.

Longing is an extreme case of loneliness. It is in this phase that you are searching for someone or making yourself open to anyone or anything to fulfil that desire. This longing then leads to lingering, which will lead you to linger around places and people to increase your chances of finding someone. Some people begin to go to extreme measures to be noticed like dating websites or even lowering their standards to match more suitors. This lingering then leads to latching; now you are latched onto someone, and now your new loneliness state of mind feels validated and in its validation begins to brew up **infatuation**. This phase is when you can't be told anything. You see all the red flags but ignore them because you feel validated in your new man or woman. Once in this state, you **lose** yourself, time, purity, innocence, self-worth, money etc. It's not worth it to marry out of the need for companionship. God's timing is perfect! God knows what you need but also knows your management ability. God is not going to add to you a person or add to your marriage anything until you or you and your spouse grow in **stewardship**. Loneliness is a scheme of the enemy designed for you to long, linger, latch and lose. You are never alone God is with you.

Everyone:

Where are you now in your life when it comes to loneliness? Circle the one that applies to you and write in the box below why?						
Mind State →	Content	Lonely	Longing	Lingering	Latching	Losing

Why are you in the state of mind?

What do you need to do to loosen yourself from the effects of loneliness?

Why is being content in God important for your future or current relationship?

Wholeness

Wholeness is the key to the success of any relationship. It is important for us to be whole before we endeavor to hold anything. Anything or anyone we try to hold without being whole we will eventually hurt or abuse. So many people start relationships, businesses, ministries etc. without being whole. Wholeness doesn't mean perfection it means prepared. A whole chair is a chair prepared and able to hold a person when they sit. A whole cup is a cup prepared and able to hold a beverage. A whole person is a person prepared and able to hold a marriage, career, ministry, parenthood etc. God wants us to be whole before we hold. So many people focus so much on the fruit they want to bear that they forget about themselves as a branch. Big fruit requires strong branches. Marriage requires strong branches. Running a business requires strong branches. Running a ministry

45

requires strong branches. Anything you desire to do and anyone you desire to be with or are currently with needs you to be a strong branch. Big fruit on weak branches breaks weak branches. A marriage, a business, a ministry will always break people who are not whole. Are you truly prepared for what you desire? Do you match what you are asking for? God only gives significant things to stewards. He only gives significant others, significant amounts of money and resources and a significant amount of responsibility to **stewards**. What kind of steward are you? Never forget that God's timing is always closest to those that are whole and are consistent with staying whole. So many people cry out that they are ready, but God doesn't care about how ready you are he cares about how long you can **stay** ready.

There is a phrase that I have heard many people say that they are either looking for their better half or their wife/ husband is their better half. Half of anything is broken. Do not look for a better half look for an **equal whole**. Don't call your significant other your better half call them your equal whole. The Psychologically of these terms will affect you. Saying better half implies that you can stay the way you are and don't have to improve but saying an equal whole suggest self-examination and significant other examination. It leads you to ask are we equal and are we whole? It leads you to examine the person you want to be with and/or if you match what you desire. Are you whole? Are you endeavoring to be so? Don't add someone else to your dysfunction if you are single and if you love the person you are with do what it takes to become whole for them.

Everyone:

What do you desire to hold? Write down below all of the things you desire to hold in your life like a marriage, children, a business etc. and write beside it if you are whole enough to hold it. In the last box write down what you need to do to hold what you are not prepared enough to hold now.

What would you like to hold and/or what are you holding now + and are you whole enough to hold them?	
I Want to hold or I am holding	Whole or not whole enough
1	
2	
3	
4	
5	
6	
7	
8	
9	
10	
11	
12	
How many of the items above are you not whole enough to hold at the moment →	#
What must you do to hold these things correctly?	

Self-awareness

In order to get ready and to stay ready, you have to be self-aware. Many people are more aware of others than they are of themselves. They tend to the business of everyone else but their own. How can you help your business succeed if you are too consumed with everyone else's? Self-awareness is a conscious knowledge of your character, feelings, motives, and desires. A person, who is self-aware, can feel the temperature and the texture of his or her own character, feelings, motives and desires. These four things are key to success. I have to always be aware of my character because my character will ensure how long I stay at a desired place. Charisma may be able to get me to the top, but it is my character, that will ensure I stay there. I have to always check to see how I handle things, how I think about things and what I am allowing to influence me because all of these things are shaping the man that I am. I have to always be aware of my feelings. I have to always check the temperature of how I feel about the current affairs of my life whether high or low. I cannot just know how I feel about a person or a thing I have to know why. Self-awareness is not just having the ability to know what I am feeling but to know why I feel it. So many people only stop at what but never address the why. I have to also be self- aware of my motives and desires. I have to always ask myself why I am pursuing this or that and I always have to make sure that I am harboring the heart of God in pursuing any aspirations. Being self-aware helps you track where you are in life. Whenever you are more aware of someone else's character, feelings motives or desires you hurt yourself or if you pursue a relationship or start a business or ministry and are completely unaware of who you are you will have the capacity to hurt you and everyone/ thing that is connected to you.

What defines you? What are the good, bad and ugly things that defines you right now? Whatever those things are you need to address them. You need to take some time to really assess your character, feelings, motives and desires and ask yourself am I truly ready to take on the next level of my life whether single or married? Am I whole enough to hold my future? Being self-aware will help you navigate your life effectively. It will help you see what to avoid, what to address and what to allow access into your life.

Everyone: How is your character, feelings, motives and desires?

How is your character →	Poor	Ok	Good
In what areas are you exhibiting poor character?	Why is having good character in a relationship important?		What do you need to do to build a good character?

What is the temperature of your feelings? Write down below all of the feelings you feel frequently and circle the temperature of those feelings and write down below how they could affect what you endeavor to hold?

Feelings	Cold	Warm	Hot
1	Cold	Warm	Hot
2	Cold	Warm	Hot
3	Cold	Warm	Hot
4	Cold	Warm	Hot
5	Cold	Warm	Hot

How are the hot feelings affecting what you are currently holding and how could they affect what you endeavor to hold?

Motives and Desires:

Write down your top aspirations and/ or the people you are/ desire to be connected to and beside them place a check for what kind of motives you have for them.			
Aspirations + People	Bad Motives	Indifferent Motives	Good Motives
1			
2			
3			
4			
5			
6			
7			
Reflect:			

Access Levels.

This topic seems to make it to each one of my books because of its importance. Right now, you have certain people, perspectives and influences that you have granted access into your life. Whatever you allow access to your life will determine the success of your life. Your access levels boil down to the level of your self-love. You right now either love yourself, hate yourself or are somewhere in between. **Self-love leads to self-care and self-hate leads to self-harm**. Those that love themselves accurately cherish their time, space, and focus. Those that struggle with self-hate will allow the wrong influences into their lives due to their insecurities. Not everyone deserves access to you.

You are very valuable to God, and He loves you tremendously. He doesn't want you to allow everyone access to you because he knows that not everyone can handle valuable people. So many people right now struggle with self-hate; they don't like who they are, how they look, and they allow themselves to be devalued due to envy and jealousy. No one on the earth is like you. You are (you)nique.

Don't allow yourself to be compared to anyone. You should only compare yourself to two people; Jesus and your old self. Comparing yourself to Jesus will keep you humble and comparing yourself to your old self will inspire you to to improve. Comparing yourself to anyone else will shortchange you because his or her path is not your path. You must always remain consciously aware of what you are allowing access to you because whomever you allow close to you could determine what doors close and open for you. I always paint this picture when talking about access levels. → There are people you will talk to on the sidewalk in front of your house, but you won't allow them access to your yard. There are some people you allow access to your yard to play with the dog or outside with your kids, but you won't allow them on your front porch. There are some people you will sit on the front porch with and sip lemonade, but you won't allow them in your living room. There are some people you will allow in your living room, but you won't allow in your bedroom. Each level is an access point. The most valuable and vulnerable place in your home is your bedroom, and the least valuable or vulnerable place is the sidewalk in front of your home. It's sad that so many people allow sidewalk status people clearance to their bedroom.

You deserve better. **Why give your body to someone who doesn't match your spirit?** You want a spirit mate, not a soul mate. The only mate for your depraved soul is Jesus, and from his work in your life, he will match you with a spirit mate. Even Jesus had access points. There were the Pharisees, the crowd, the 70, the 9, the 3 and the Father. Each of these individuals he dealt with differently. He dealt with the Pharisees **strictly**, the crowd **empathetically**, the 70 and the 9 disciples **specifically**, the three disciples **closely** and the father **intimately**. The most important relationship to Jesus in this equation was the Heavenly Father. For you to deal with each relationship group accurately and maturely, you must engage with your heavenly father. Talking to him daily, reading daily, fasting often, serving constantly will open your eyes to his heart and to every engagement, you have.

He will show you that in life you will only have three solid friends where you can transfigure and show everything to without judgment. He will show you that you will have a core team of 12 and an outer team of 70 whether in your ministry, business or career that will help support you but be watchful of Judas' because they creep in when things are small and knowingly or unknowingly try to cheat you. He will also tell you not to confuse any of these 9 or more individuals to your core three. He will also teach you to only give the crowd your love but not your heart because the crowd can only handle the expressions of your love but are unable to handle the fears, failures and the frustrations of your heart. He will teach you to only give your haters (the Pharisees), the truth without debate and don't allow their criticisms to affect your heart because what they want is control over how Christ wants you to live. A person's reaction will always let you know their motives. Let God determine everyone's access points.

Do you love you? Do you like you?

The answers to these questions will determine how quickly you allow someone access to you. What is it that you do not like about yourself? Whatever you do not like about yourself if it can change, change it, if it cannot, accept it because the quicker you accept, the quicker it can't be used against you. Satan will always use what you like and hate most about yourself against you. He will make you vain about the things you like about yourself, or he will cause you to be vulnerable about the things you hate about yourself. For me, there were two things I hated about myself one was my forehead the other was my weight. My weight was during my later years, and my forehead was during my earlier years. I use to as a kid go through great measures to hide the slope of my forehead. I would wear toboggans I would wrinkle my forehead to make it look better in pictures I just hated it because I was getting all kinds of big head jokes. I was the person people practiced their big head jokes on. But one day in my mid teenage years, I talked to my mom, and she said this "you better accept it son because you can't change it. - Why hide what you cannot change" and from that moment I stopped hiding what was uniquely me. Every time I got a big joke, I would simply say I have a bigger brain than you do lol. Looking back at it that was a corny comeback, but it worked for me! Since I could not change my forehead, I just accepted it.

Now let's talk about what I had the power to change. During my late 20's I went through a rough season of depression. I lost my identity as a preacher and was overwhelmed with the pressures of life. During this time, I gained so much weight. I went from 225lbs to 315lbs. I was drowning in the pool of emotional eating, and I hated myself. One day while walking the track outside of one of the YMCA's in Charlotte with my now fiancé I realized that I could change this. I didn't want to feel horrible every night while trying to fall asleep or feeling like I could die at any moment. So I told myself that if lost it once before I can definitely lose it again. From that day forward I stopped going to Bo jangles (sad face), I stopped going to Jack in the Box, I stopped eating honey buns and I started going to Whole Foods and cooking, and at this moment I am 70lbs lighter. Both things I did not like one I accepted the other I rejected. Change what you can change and own what you cannot change.

Right now, what have you yet to own about yourself? What frustrations are you causing your husband or wife because you have yet to accept what you need to accept and reject what you need to reject? Marriage was designed to be a gift, not a burden it was designed to be a happy place not a centerpiece of your hope.

Everyone: How do you feel about you?

What do you like about you?	What do you not like about you?
1	1
2	2
3	3
4	4
5	5
6	6
7	7
What can you change?	What can you not change?
1	1
2	2
3	3
4	4
5	5
6	6
7	7
How could feeling negatively about yourself affect your future or current relationship?	

Access Levels:

Who has access to you at this moment of your life? - Family members, friends, influencers etc.	Do they deserve access: Yes or no?
1	
2	
3	
4	
5	
6	
7	
8	
9	
10	
11	
12	

How's your relationship with the father →	Non-existent.	Poor	Ok	Great
In what ways could it improve?				

Who's your core 3 (Best Friends)
1
2
3

Who are your 9-70?	Who is in your crowd?	Who are your haters?

People Placement: Utilize this page to log the people in your life right now and the people you will eventually meet as you journey throughout life. Let this page be a reminder of where you should place certain people in your life. Beside each name list why they belong there.

The Fence: People who don't deserve any access to you.	
Name	Why
1	
2	
3	
4	
5	

The Front Yard: Neighbors, Associates etc.	
Name	Why
1	
2	
3	
4	
5	

The Front Porch: Good or new people that you still have an eye on	
Name	Why
1	
2	
3	
4	
5	

The Front Room: Family and proven friends	
Name	Why
1	
2	
3	
4	
5	

For Intimacy Only: Your Spouse and Children	
Name	Why
1	
2	
3	
4	

Before you date!

Preparation and Purity of heart are key to success. For us to handle the mature components of love, we have to understand mastery and motives. Let us first look at Preparation

There are four areas of preparation

1. Personal Preparation
2. Purpose Preparation
3. Partner Preparation
4. Partnership Preparation

Personal Preparation

You are the sum of your habits. Your habits will determine who and what you will become. So many people take their potential for granted. They think that everything by the sure act of waiting and whining will be granted to them, but that's not the case. You are your greatest project. Imagine the person you could be; better yet imagine the person God desires for you to be. His purpose for you is so great, and all you have to do to fulfil it is to trust him and prepare. I want to become every ounce of who God wants me to be, and I want to fulfill everything he wants me to do. I don't want to live my whole life and find out from God that I didn't even scratch the surface. I want to stand before my maker and hear the sweet words well done. It's going to be crazy how many people are going to hear from God partially done or not done at all. Your level of preparation will determine how much of your purpose you will tap into. But how can you tap into your full purpose if you are not plugged into the presence of God? God's presence is the best place on earth. His presence is the best presence even if it's in the jungles of Asia or Africa, or in a single parent home of three burrowed deep in a crime infested neighborhood, or in a New York Jail cell. No matter how bad the place is if his presence is there it's a great place. So many people want lands and buildings but don't want to be or build where God is. Any relationship or marriage that does not honor God will self-destruct. Any relationship that does not have two prepared individuals will self-destruct in some way. To prepare you must be in the presence of God, and you must know what he wants you to do. Once you know what you are to do you will need to prepare accordingly. Life is not going to make it easy for you. Preparing for anything is difficult it takes discipline. Without a sense of destiny, nothing desired can be accomplished.

Since this is a book on resources for date nights, let's talk specifically on the process of preparing for dating or courting. For those that are married I will discuss some points for you all in a few but for the singles here are nine things you must do if you desire to date for destiny

1. Delight
2. Devote
3. Desire (divine or distracted)
4. Decide
5. Destroy
6. Detail
7. Discipline
8. Develop
9. Depend

The word destiny means a place of fulfilled promises; a season of purpose in action. When it comes to marriage, we should all desire for our marriage to be a place of destiny; a place of fulfilled promises and a place where purpose is in action. I know for me, I do not want my first 3 years of marriage to be hell on earth I want it to be help on earth. I do not want it to be arguments galore I want it to be filled with purpose and passion. I want it to be where God is at work. However, for a marriage to be a place of destiny we have to assess what we delight in. whatever has your delight has your devotion. The bible says to delight yourself in the lord and he will give you the desires of your heart. This scripture is telling us that when we delight in or find our greatest joy in God, he will give us the desires of our hearts. He is not going to answer the desires of a heart that does not delight in him. So many people want Gods hand but not his heart. You get to his hand by going through his heart but not too many people want to go that route. When you truly love him more than anything or have the heart to do so your desires will naturally match his desires and you will only want what he wants because receiving anything that is not from him will only separate you from him.

A person that delights in the lord as their provider, priest and protector will live a life devoted. Devotion is key. The process of desiring what God desires begins with devotion. Serving God is an honor and when we serve him with our whole heart, our desires over time will begin to change and we will begin to hear his heartbeat and discern his thoughts and his assignments, and our desires will mature. Who I am at 32 and what I desire now is 10 x's different than what my desires were at 22. Bet at 22 I loved God, but my desires weren't mature. My heart at 22 was lustful, prideful just downright filthy it was tainted but as I matured and grew in God my desires changed. Even what type of woman I wanted to marry has matured it went from the focus of how shapely she was to how shaped her heart is. What I am saying is that my increased devotion to God changed what I desired. Don't get me wrong I still desire the same things like success, marriage, respect and influence but the reasons why I desire them are different; instead of me receiving glory, I simply want God to be glorified. God follows the Glory road. He cares about why we grind. If we grind for our glory, we will perish but if we grind for his glory we will have life everlasting.

A God focused desire naturally puts a line in the sand. It separates what needs to go and what needs to stay. When we delight in God and begin to devote more time with him, we begin to see our sins for what they really are and our hearts for what it really is. When I saw pornography for what it really was, in the midst of my devotion with God, I had to make a decision. See I need the anointing to be effective. I cannot faithfully practice habitual sins and expect God to move through me in a mighty way consistently. There is a big difference between talent and anointing. Everyone has talent but not everyone's talents are anointed. So many people mix up the two - they think that the mastery of their talent is anointing but all it is; is just talent. The anointing is Gods hand on your talent. It is His hand on your voice, your mind, your strategy and your gifting. I don't want to be a talented preacher I want to be an anointed preacher because it is not the talent that destroys the yoke it's the anointing on the talent that does. I want to be an anointed husband and anointed father and none of this is possible without deep devotion with God and deciding to destroy any and everything that will separate me from Him. What is in the way of Gods hand being on you and his power consistently flowing through you?

The state of your devotion with God will determine what you will need to destroy. Destroying things about ourselves may never end until we are with God, that's just how deep and depraved our hearts are. We can be good for a season, but life will test us. Life is very complex, and there are so many layers to us and as we grow and mature we will see deeper into what we will need to change. The more we devote to God the clearer life becomes. The health of a fruit is predicated on the health of the tree and its vine. If the vine and the tree are healthy the fruit will be as well. Before we can have prosperity, we must have pruning. God always brings us through a season where we are pruned so that we can see clearly. He prunes us so that we can see the details of our lives. How detailed are you about your life?

Are you truly trying to grow and improve? Growth is in the details. If you want to be married and to have a successful one, you must focus on the details of your life. Details meaning the little things, it means looking for the little foxes that spoils the vine. It is the little things that trips us up the most. It's the little things that we allow to grow into bigger things that causes our downfall. See little foxes are no direct threat to the fruit because the fruit is too high, but they are a big threat to the vine, which is the source of the fruit. The little things that we overlook eat away at our dependency on the vine. Jesus said I am the vine and we are the branches the little things we overlook now slowly disconnect us to our ultimate source. What are those little things in your life right now keeping you from growing in an area? Don't you want to be the best man, woman, husband, wife and parent that you can be? Parenthood and marriage-hood requires whole men and whole women. Your future needs for you to daily focus on growth. A detailed-minded person naturally becomes a disciplined person. The fruit from discipline is always sweeter than the immediate fruit of laziness. I would rather reap later from discipline than to reap immediately from procrastination or laziness. The more detailed minded you are, the more disciplined you become and the more you naturally develop the better the chances your marriage or your purpose will thrive. Ball players who become champions or perineal all-stars maximize their offseason. They put in the work in the gym to ensure they succeed when its game time. They look at the film, they analyze their competition, they look at their percentages and they take that information into the gym, and improve on those areas. Your offseason or singleness is a gift; it's a season to prepare not just for marriage but for your overall purpose in life. The more we develop, the more of a service we can become to others. Once you have done all these things and are flowing in these principles daily all you have left to do is **depend**.

There is nothing worst, than to do all of these things, embrace your growth, reap the fruit of your disciplines and then depend on you and not God. The most important point in these D's is **dependency**. No matter how much you grow, improve or bear fruit you must still depend on God for your promotion. Growth attracts and sometimes it attracts bad and good things. You will be more attractive to women, to men and you will be more attractive to opportunities, but you must still depend on God. The bible says that promotion does not come from the east or from the west but it comes from above. You must still trust God on who you are supposed to be with. Dating should not be in your hands but in your dependency on God. He knows who's best for you, and he knows how to mold you into the best person for the person he has for you. Before you date someone else, date you. Set dates to develop, set dates to grow so that when you are married, you will be who God wants you to be and you will be able to submit to or sacrifice for your partner. If

- your delight is not in God,
- you are not deepening your devotion to him,
- your desires are not his desires
- you haven't decided to destroy your sins,
- you are not focused on the details of your life,
- you are not disciplining yourself to develop
- or trusting your dependency on God

then you are **not** ready to date anyone. A breakdown in any one of the areas can cause dangerous effects in your relationship.

On a scale between 1-10 how is your delight in God?	#
Why this number?	

What are the things you desire most in your life and do they find their roots in your delight in God?	
Desires	Yes or No

In what ways can you deepen your devotion to God?

What sins need to be destroyed in your life and what must you do to destroy them?

What are the detailed things in your life you need to focus more on? What are the thing little things tripping you up right now?

Where could you be more disciplined and it what areas do you need to depend on God more?

Purpose Preparation

Purpose is the name of the game. Each one of us has a purpose, but the sad thing is, not too many of us are pursuing it with **urgency**. Life is a vapor and it must be taken seriously. Now I am not saying you cannot enjoy your life but some of us are enjoying too much of it to the point that we are ineffective when it comes to being who we are supposed to be in this realm. Before you can prepare to be with someone, you have to prepare for your purpose and know exactly what it is.

My next book will cover more about this topic and I have a ton of videos on YouTube that covers this more in-depth you can go there now and just type in Purpose Joshua Eze, and most of my videos on purpose will pop up.

It is Important to know and prepare for your purpose in stages. There is a purpose for every stage of your life. There was a purpose for the last stage a purpose for the stage you are on now, and a purpose for the next stage and you have to always remain tuned into God to know how to function on your current stage and how to prepare for the next one. For instance, I know my scope. I know I'm going to be a travelling church planter and I know that I am going to influence some pillars of culture and by me knowing that I must eat, sleep, think, play, and prepare like it. Your level of preparation will determine how much of your purpose you do at a high level, all of us show glimpses of who we are when talking with a friend or randomly with a stranger but a lot of us don't get the opportunity to function in our purpose at a **high level**. I remember one morning I was getting up and I heard God say to record my first YouTube/ Facebook video. I was feeling very insecure that morning and was like who is going to want to watch me? Before that day I was only doing audio/ podcast messages and blogs, and I was comfortable with that, but on this day, God was leading me to record videos. This was right when YouTube was coming on the scene, so technology wasn't like it is today; there were no Facebook lives, Periscopes and I sure didn't have an iPhone back then so I went and got my old camcorder, the one I used to use in college to Skype, and started recording.

I didn't know that me switching to video would lead me to a place where I am currently with 45k subscribers on YouTube and my videos being watched in over 100 countries. I say all this to say this → don't allow fear to cripple you from functioning in your purpose at the level you were created to function at. So many people either allow fear to cripple them or the fact that they don't have all the perfect conditions in place to cripple them. As I always say don't wait for perfect conditions to start something just use the conditions you have perfectly. God wants you to engage with him and his purpose for you now so that your failures and your resistances will shape you. I am 10x's better now than I was in 2009 but what if I didn't engage, what if I didn't attempt would you even be reading this book now? So many people are working at jobs looking out of their window thinking about the what if's. I don't want to be a what if I did kind of person I want to be a look at what I did kind through God kind of person. How can you take a potential mate seriously if you haven't taken your purpose seriously? You must daily work on your craft and grow in your purpose so that you will be able to recognize who God sends for you to marry or to partner with.

Partner Preparation

Personal and partner preparation go hand in hand. Once I know who I am in Christ, who I am to others and who I am to myself I will now be aware of how to prepare for a partner. The good thing about us believers if we choose to accept it is that we don't have to worry about finding or being found by "the one". If we are connected to the One and he is number one in our lives we don't have to worry about who the one is. So many people settle outside of the will of God that they don't get the chance to see Gods original will but have to settle for his redemptive will. Meaning now you are in a relationship with a person that wasn't for you or outside of Gods timing, and now through repentance, you have to trust that he will redeem it all. I want Gods original plan and I am sure you do too. With that being said, we do not have to worry about when or who we just have to focus on the assignment at hand not the assignments in his hands.

Once I know who I am, and know what I am called to, I can now prepare. For instance, if you are a single woman and you desire to match a healthy eating, workout warrior, God-fearing man then you will aim to prepare to serve such a man. You will work on your healthy cooking skills, you will go to the gym you will seek Gods word on how to serve a man of God and you will begin to practice daily for this man. If you are a single man and you desire a fun loving, adventurous, God-fearing, healthy eating, shapely workout queen then you will begin to practice habits that will help sustain her adventurous and healthy lifestyle. So many people pray for a person they don't match and wonder why the one they want don't latch. Disciplined individuals only latch onto to people that match their disciplines. Undisciplined and insecure people latch onto anything. A mature person will wait however long for Gods timing but an immature person will settle out of impatience. Write down who you are right now not the person you say you want to be but the person you are, and I want you to really write down beside it the person you currently match. This reality check will let you know who you are mature enough to handle. I want you to be honest about your spiritual, emotional, mental and physical maturity and see exactly who you are mature enough to match. This reality check should inspire you to improve. Don't ask God for something you don't match.

*Do the exercise above on another sheet of paper.

Partnership preparation – Divine Connections

Along the path of your destiny are dots; divine dots designed to connect you to people, places and perspectives to help you fulfil your destiny if you so choose to observe them. It is vitally important that we discern the spaces that we are in because any place could house a divine don't or connection in them. I always live by the rule to treat everyone with respect despite race, class, orientation or gender because you never know who holds the code or the dot to your next level. I am where I am today because of how I nurture my relationships, and you are where you are based on how well you nurtured yours. So many people burn bridges and don't even know that they are shutting themselves out from a potential opportunity.

Who you may feel like you don't need now you may need later. Partiality has stifled a lot of people's potential. Not all dots on your path are black, white, yellow, Christian or straight they are different colors, and God will use anyone to promote you. Was the Pharaoh that promoted Joseph a believer? Was the King that promoted Daniel a believer? No; they weren't, but they were used for the glory of God. You must treat the poor as you would the rich. You must treat the one in the baggie clothes like the one in the corporate suit because you never know who knows your future wife, husband, employer, loan officer, angel investor or lifesaver. You must prepare to treat everyone with dignity because when it all boils down to it the only ism that matters is Salvationism; not racism or classism. The question isn't are you rich or are you poor or if you are black or if you are white it all boils down to are you saved or are you not are you regenerate or are you not. The unity in Godhead with the Father, Son and the Holy Spirit is the only person that can teach us to not only be one with ourselves (spirit, soul and body) but to also be one with each other. Right now, in America so many people only see black dots or white dots or red dots (Republican) or blue dots (democrats) or straight dot or rainbow dots and we're all systematically being separated to stifle the organic purposes of unity. We all need each other and love is the language that connects us. If we don't prepare to be connected, we will die due to tribalism or isolationism. Prepare to be connected because you never know who you will meet that God will use to promote you. Love everyone!

Accountability

You are only as good as your accountability. Every area of your life must have someone that can hold you accountable in that area. You need people to help hold your strengths and your weaknesses accountable. Any area that lacks accountability will cause you to fall.

Four stages of growth

There are four stages of growth

1. Information
2. Inspiration
3. Preparation
4. Demonstration

Each of these areas are key to growing and sustaining growth. Let's look first at information. So many people in our world today are misinformed and its systematic. The enemy does not want us to be informed about any form of truth, and even if we know the truth, he wants us too lazy to act it out. Information opens the doors to opportunities. When a person is informed, they have the intangible resources they need to change their lives and potentially the lives of others. The problem lies in the hands of those that restrain the information. This system was designed to have you distracted with information that doesn't matter. They want you to prioritize your life focused mostly on the least sources of info. I believe that for you to succeed, you must desire to know what needs to be known not what you would like to know. For instance, everyone needs to know who the creator is. No one should pursue anything significant until they know intellectually and emotionally who designed them and this place called earth. That truth holds the key to every jail cell we are in. When we know who created us, we will know what for and when we know what for we will walk in a freedom that's unheard of. Do you know who created you and what he created you for? The answers to these questions are paramount and you must know these answers before you endeavor to start a marriage, a family, a business or a ministry. The enemy wants to keep this information away because if you connect to it and pursue it you will be a torch that enlightens others.

Once a person is informed, there is a sense of inspiration that births. When a person is informed about their health, about their lost family member, about them being able to accomplish an assignment Inspiration births. Inspiration is the match information sparks. It is the fuel that starts the engine it's the first step towards a new goal! Every time I look in a child's eyes at the school I work at, I always endeavor to plant a seed of information into them that will inspire them. So many of our children and adults are fully capable of doing what they were created to do they are just not inspired. That is why it is important for us to be vocal about our experiences and to show them how possible it is but if everyone is stuck in a place they were not created for and are miserable, how can anybody be inspired?

Deep inspiration leads to the desire to prepare. When a person catches a glimpse of who they were created to be and embraces the possibilities they have in Christ to accomplish it they will do whatever it takes to prepare for it. I'm so glad God showed me a glimpse of who I am going to be to this world. Many nights I lay awake trying to remember it in detail, and when I am sucked into the scenes of my future, I can't help but say Josh you are the greatest, Josh you will accomplish every bit of this, Josh you need to do this to get there etc. I begin to speak it and believe it even on my toughest days. That is important because inspiration without preparation is pointless.

So many people are inspired but not inspired deeply enough. Deep inspiration turns into thorough preparation and thorough preparation leads to empowered demonstration. One of my fondest memories with my dad was when we would hangout and he would always remind me of what my last name meant. My last name Eze means King or Kang depending on where you are from lol. But he would tell me it doesn't matter what anyone says about you, you are a king! The older I got I believed it and began to demonstrate it in my walk; in my shoulders in my words and I began to demonstrate it even when there was nothing royal around me. I began to embrace the fact that every environment that I walk in will be a product of me not me a product of it. There is nothing a white man or a black man can say that can shake me off of who I am in Christ. I have to embrace who I am in Him so that I can demonstrate what it is to be a man, a husband, a father, and a leader. We need more godly demonstrations of what it means to be the various components of being a human, but none of this is possible if we are not godly informed, godly inspired and godly prepared. What are you demonstrating now? What kind of man, woman, wife, husband, father, mother or leader are you presenting? Everyone one is demonstrating these things; the problem is most are not due to a lack of proper information, due little to no inspiration and due to laziness. How bad do you want to demonstrate the person God created you to be?

Pure Motives

Mastery is one-fold the other fold are motives. God cares more about why you do things versus what you did. People may only be able to see your charitable actions, but it is God that sees the motives behind them. Actions reflect the actor's heart. Good actions may touch many lives, but it is the motives of the heart that touches God. Before you get into a dating relationship with anyone you must have a pure heart. Let's look at some points that will help us produce a consistent pure life.

Pure Points

For us to live a genuine life, we must have a

1. Pure Helper
2. Pure Head
3. Pure Heart
4. Pure Habits
5. Pure Hands

Pure Helper

We all are influenced by something. Most of our perspectives, feelings, habits and ways have been passed down by people we mirror the most. Before I elaborate further let me first explain the difference between pure and perfect. God doesn't intend for us to live perfectly just purely. A perfect life is a life without error a pure life is a life that knows how to either avoid error or rebound from it. There was only one person that ever walked this realm, that was perfect and that was Jesus. He lived the life we were supposed to live and died our death so that we can have the opportunity to live pure. Purity = Honesty, Purity = Integrity, Purity = Process and that process is the sanctification work of Christ. Once we accept the pure Gospel, we are now sparked to grow into a pure person. But in order for this to formulate into our lives, we have to make sure we have pure help. The purest help we have is the Holy Spirit. He is the one that we should be asking for help the most. His leading and help will help us discern the proper external help. The Holy Spirit is a gentle leader. He will never force us to do anything. It is our responsibility to follow him and it is our responsibility to guard ourselves from all carnal and non-beneficial influences. It's crazy the shows we watch, the music we listen too, the voices we respect. We believe that these influences don't influence us that much, but they do. Your mind is a sponge and it will soak in anything you entertain the most. Entertained is such a dangerous word. Its definition is in the word "Enter the detained" whatever we allow ourselves to watch or listen to if we are not careful will detain us into a trance like state and drop its agenda into our minds causing us to be conformed to the image of their agenda. The Holy Spirt is a comforter not a detainer. It is his responsibility to point us to the greatest image, Jesus, to lead us towards that image and to help us recognize who we should allow to influence us. When we need help, we need to seek the Holy Spirit first. Before you consult your external counsel, consult your internal counsel.

The Holy Spirits pure help will help us to have a pure mind and a pure heart. Our heart and head were designed to work together. Our mind was designed to guard our heart and stabilize its emotions. If our minds are not being renewed, how can we expect our emotions to be stabilized? Our minds right now are either being conformed into an image or transformed into an image and it all boils down to the images we emulate. The architects of this satanic system knows the effects of distorted images. If you want to destroy people remove important images and replace them with incompetent images. Remove God, the correct image of the family, the correct image of sexuality, modesty etc. and replace it with distorted images and flood the media with these images utilizing actors and deceive the masses into bearing these images. When God is removed, and his image of every sector of life is removed or ridiculed, then you will have a bunch of people living contrary to the original image.

God cares about our mental and emotional health. He cares about how we think and how we feel. How pure is your mind and your emotions? What influences are you accepting? What do you think about God, money, sexual purity, life etc.? How you think about these things will determine how you feel about these things and how you feel about these things will determine your habits. A Pure life needs pure habits. Impure habits are conceived by carnal desires triggered by carnal images. The enemy wants your habits. If he can have your habits then he can have access to your time, resources, money and family. He knows all I have to do is to get you to taste sex, drugs, "freedom" and temporal success and have you become a feign off it utilizing these things to contaminate everything connected to you. So many people want to be freed from God but fail to realize that everyone is a slave. We are either slaves or bondservants of Jesus or satan. For us to be pure individuals, we must audit our habits and examine why we are connected to people and things. Impure habits will lead to the misuse of things with our hands both privately and publicly. The enemy wants access to every key part of you - he wants access to your eyes and ears hoping to have them latch or listen to one of his carnal images. He wants access to the filter of your mind so that he can have you think impure thoughts about the opposite sex, about other people groups and success so that you will allow them to take root in your heart. He wants access to your heart so that you will think with your feelings instead of thinking biblically. He wants your irrationality to fuel your erratic emotions causing you to become overly attached to clouded views, carnal values etc. He wants access to your habits and hands so that you too will express an image, that is ungodly and inflict harm on those that cannot help but be influenced by you. He just wants us to remain impure and reach for deeper places of impurity.

Matthew 5:8 says blessed are the pure in heart for they shall see God. Impure people will not see God. Some imperfect will but not the impure. Our hearts must always be guarded, and all of our thoughts must be audited because if not we will die with the image of the world on us and not see God. There are so many unconverted people in our fellowships not because they were drawn there to repent and be baptized, but they were drawn there through marketing schemes and stamped with a distorted image of Christianity. Anyone truly converted by God cannot stay impure for long; there will be an innate desire to change. Today's Christianity has done a horrible job of presenting the image of the full gospel - all we see is a partial gospel. The perfect image of the gospel is God's love and God's wrath. We won't be able to appreciate his love until we understand his coming wrath. His wrath is hovering over everyone who is harboring iniquity in his or her heart. His wrath will be released on everyone that bore his name unregenerately and will consume each person that is not truly converted. Hell is going to be full of lip serviced Christians, Christians that only confessed but never was converted. Until we accept the pure, image of Jesus into our lives and allow that image to

- transform our thinking,
- evoke confessions and repentance from our hearts,
- renew impure habits and cleanse our sins,

then we will always remain impure. No relationship can survive with impure influences, thinking, feelings, habits and hands - it just won't.

How bad do you want to prepare for the next level? Are you sure you are ready? Are you sure the person you are courting is ready? Don't allow infatuation to cloud your judgment.

For those that are married.

The pursuit never ends. Your wife and your husband is a human and being a human is complicated. We each have different upbringings, perspectives and values that when touched, requires the patience of those that love us to help us get through it. You know the issues in your home, and I'm sure you can trace them all the way back to the point it was conceived. Sometimes looking backwards will give us the perspective and the patience we need to empathize going forward. It seems that what is missing out of many relationships is **empathy**. There are many expectations but very little empathy.

The height of an expectation is only proven too high when someone else proves it to be so. In our minds we think many of our expectations are valid but if we're honest not a lot of them are. Now I am not talking about the basic expectations that holds a relationship together, but the unnecessary hoops you put him through and the unnecessary and unrealistic expectations you put on her. Many of us are expecting from our spouses what we are not expecting from ourselves. When you match your expectations watch it inspire your spouse too especially if God is involved. Selfless love is what keeps relationships sailing, and selfish love is what causes them to sink. If you are harboring any selfishness, then you are playing a part in the fall of your relationship. There is a big difference between self-care and selfishness. Self-care is the correct way to be in a relationship, but when self-care is out of balance, it turns into selfishness; a mind state that expresses that everything centers around you. You are not the **earth** and everything doesn't revolve around you. Everything under the firmament was designed to assist and to help you. We were created to serve each other. Love is best when you love without expectation and when you love without always thinking about you. That's why it's important to be in a relationship or marriage with someone who is completely submitted to God because you can serve, serve, serve knowing that God will prick their heart to serve you and they will oblige.

***

Throughout the next few pages you will have the opportunity to reflect on your personal life as well as your dating/ married life. All of the questions in my game Dating prep are listed below with spaces for you to answer. Feel free to do it by yourself or with your significant other. I pray the content helps you and your marriage evolve for the glory of God! Have Fun Preparing!

Family Tree

1. What is your mom's name? Cloud
2. What is your dad's name? Cloud

Self-explanatory. A person's name is the foundation they build on; knowing their names will help you start the process of getting to know his or her family.

| Their Moms Name: |
| Their Dads Name: |
| Your Moms Name: |
| Your Dad's Name: |

3. Who raised you and how was your experience? Cloud and Cement

The person that raised him or her were the main ones responsible for shaping them. It is important for you to know who raised them or what was allowed to raise them in their home. Knowing a person's experiences growing up will give you insight into who they are now. Take the time to listen to them and see how they act when talking about their past. Forgiveness is the best foundation to build on not un-forgiveness. If they seem to be still affected by how they were raised or seem to have resentment towards their guardian, then you might want to proceed with caution. Solid relationships require people to grow from the soil of forgiveness not unforgiveness. Resentment is not the best motivation forgiveness is. Healed people heal people hurt people hurt people.

| Who raised them: |
| How was their experience? |

Who raised you:
How was your experience:

4. Which family elder are you closest to and why? Cloud
5. Who were you closest to growing up and why? Cloud

Whoever they were the closest too growing up will determine what they will have in their closet. We reflect who we are the closest too and many people have adopted habits from their closest family member or friends. This question will help you see deeper into who passed down the wardrobe your significant other is wearing internally now.

Who were their closest family members or friends growing up?	How did they influence them?

Who were your closest family members or friends growing up?	How did they influence you?

6. How close are you to each parent? Cloud

There is a saying I often say "If you show me your family I can show you your foundation" every person has a foundation the question though is how sturdy is that foundation? Take your time to hear who they were closest to and see how they may have rubbed off on them. Also, make sure to analyze the effects of them being in a single parent or a two parent home and remember not all single parent homes were bad and not all two-parent homes were good.

What kind of family did they grow up with and how did it affect them? (Single or both parent)
Which parent were they closest to and why?

What kind of family did you grow up with and how is it affecting you now?

Which parent were you closest to and why?

Family Traditions

7. What are some of your family traditions? Cloud
8. How much of an influence do they have on you and your relationships or other decisions? Cloud, Cement

Traditions are birth from tribes, and the tone of your partner's tribe could be passed down into your marriage. It's important for you to know what traditions he or she holds on to and the connection they have to them. Some traditions can be great, and some can have a great toll on a relationship especially if they contradict your values and principles. Have a conversation with your partner and see what kind of connection they have to their family's traditions and also see how you can connect to them because you never know their traditions could be a great asset to your relationship.

Also, make sure you or your partner are not being forceful with your traditions because not everyone had the privilege or has the patience now to embrace a foreign or different tradition. If you are with someone, you feel you will spend the rest of your life with, make sure you give them time to understand your traditions and grow into liking them. Holding on to traditions shouldn't lead you into letting go of the one you love. Just talk about it!

Their family traditions	How much of an influence do they have on them or could have on your relationships?	How could their traditions help your relationship?
Your family traditions	How much of an influence do they have on you or could have on your relationships?	How could your traditions help your relationship?

Family Attributes

9. What is a negative attribute about your family that may affect you now or in the future? Cloud, Cement
10. What's a positive attribute about your family and how will that affect your future? Cloud, Cement
11. In what ways could your upbringing affect your future relationships in a good or bad way? Cloud, Cement

Everyone right now is somewhat affected by how they were raised. Some people for the worst and some for the better. It is important for you to know how much of their childhood experience is still affecting them today especially when they are alone. Some people will use relationships to escape their childhood pains and utilize the company of others to stifle the screams of their past. Any person without ventilation will be stuffy inside. You want to be in a relationship with a person that is hollow of any bitterness and filled up with Joy. A person's perception of their past will affect your future. Make sure they have a positive one.

Also, be mindful that some people may be overly attached to their families' positive attributes like how wealthy they are, how influential they are etc. You want a person that can stand on their own two feet and not still be standing on the shoulders of their parents. Everyone's past will affect his or her future somehow; you just have to make sure that it is for the better.

Make sure you too take some time to analyze your experiences and see how they could be used against your relationship.

Their families positive attributes	How will it affect their future?
Your families positive attributes	How will it affect your future?

Significant Memories

12. What's one good memory you have of your upbringing? Cloud, Cement
13. What's one bad memory you have of your upbringing? Cloud, Cement

Memories are saved moments. Our enemy goes to great lengths to ensure we are careless with our actions because he knows every carnal unction acted upon will leave a memory. Like I've said in many videos and in my last book; significant moments will create significant memories and significant memories will fuel a significant momentum or emotion that will cause more significant movements which will, in turn, start the cycle again. You may not be able to erase a memory, but you can erase the effects of them. So many people are in relationships now with people who are still haunted by their memories, still emotional about them, causing them to be difficult to be around. You want a person that is freed from the effects of their negative or positive memories. What do they remember? What do you remember? What could be still cooking in your heart or theirs that could cause the marriage to burn down to the ground?

Memories were designed to bring joy not pain. Never forget your perception is what gives your memories power. How you see what happened will determine how you make things happen now.

What's one good memory from their upbringing?	What's one bad memory from their upbringing?
What's one good memory form your upbringing?	What's one bad memory from your upbringing?

Does the size of the family matter?

    14. How big is your family? Cloud

This question will give you insight on how either isolated or involved they were in their childhood. It will also give you an idea of how many people you will have to meet over the holiday's lol.

How big is their family →	Small	Medium	Large
How big is your family? →	Small	Medium	Large

Our Family Tree

    15. What would you like to see on our family tree? Cement, Corp
    16. What branches would we like to have on our family tree? Cement, Corp

I am sure when you saw this question you were like what is Coach Josh trying to get me to ask. Well, we all know what a family tree is but how many of us are specific on what kind of tree we want to develop. Your attention to detail is a reflection of your defined desired outcomes. If you have specific desired outcomes for your life, you will pay attention to the details that will ensure those desired outcomes are met. A person without defined desired outcomes will drift throughout life, but a person who wants to see things manifested in their life will do whatever it takes to ensure the details are in operation. What do you desire to be the outcome of your life in 5, 10 60 years? Whatever you say you must be willing to pay the detailed price for those outcomes. The sad thing is many people are quick to say what they desire but are not willing to be disciplined enough to see those desires met. Words are cheap, actions are expensive, and a fulfilled destiny is priceless. In order for your single life or relationship to be successful, you must be a person of vision. A lot of people can see but not that too many people have vision. What do you see down the road of your life? What does your spouse or fiancé see down the road for their life? Take some time to think about what you would like to see on your family tree and if you are married take some time to discuss with your spouse what you would like to see on you guys tree going forward. Below are some branches I want you to consider and I want you to be honest and put how strong the branch is now and how you plan to get it stronger or to keep it strong.

Financial Branch: Weak or Strong?

Spiritual Branch: Weak or Strong?

Creative Branch: Weak or Strong?

Integrity Branch: Weak or Strong?

Physical Health Branch: Weak or Strong?

Love Branch: Weak or Strong?

Emotional and Mental Branch: Weak or Strong?

Identity and Self-worth Branch: Weak or Strong?

Spouse and Children Branch: Weak or Strong?

Children

17. How many kids would you like to have and why? Cement, Corp
18. As a family how will we raise our children? Corp
19. What are your views on disciplining children? Corp

Children are a blessing, and your level of maturity and life balance will determine how much of a burden they will be to you and you to them. Each child deserves to be brought up in an environment that is a home and that is ready to ensure that child is raised with love and care. Now if you already have children and maybe in a single parent home I'm not saying you're no good because I am a product of a single-parent home, but as you move forward you have to make sure that you bring in a person sent by God that will be that good father or mother figure to your child. But before we can do so we must know what a mother and a father is.

A mother is a woman who nurtures, and a father is one who instructs. These two traits plus the guidance of God are important to the raising of a child. If any of these pieces are missing a child could grow up with voids and insecurities. Developing a plan on how you guys would like to raise kids before having them or while they are small is essential to you guys success. Take some time to discuss how many children you both would like to have and develop a child development/ discipline plan on how you plan on raising them. The bible says train up a child in the way they should go so when they grow old they will not depart from it.

> How do you guys plan to raise children?

A Church Family.

20. As a family, what church will we root ourselves in? Cement and Corp
21. As a family, how will we approach church and giving? Cement, Corp

Being rooted in a healthy church is important. We all need a group of people to encourage us and to hold us accountable. No church is perfect, but through God, you can be perfectly placed in one. God has a local body for you to root your family in. Take some time to pray with your spouse or future spouse and see where God wants to plant you all.

Also be alert on how attached a person is to their church. There is a big difference between being planted by God versus being planted by emotions or an agenda. If the person barks back when asked to pray on the matter, If not married, press in a little more to see why and if married, seek God privately through prayer for their sensitivity and for your wisdom and discernment moving forward. Now don't get me wrong being connected to a community is great but it can sometimes cause an unbalanced emotional attachment. God should be your source and everything else a resource. Make sure you both are not overly attached to your church because a deep attachment could really affect your relationship in the future.

Giving:

Take some time to discuss how you both plan to approach giving to your local church both financially and through volunteering. Helping a bigger cause together and contributing to the advancement of the kingdom of God can spark a new flame in your relationship.

What church do they go to? →		
What kind of attachment do they have to their church? Check Below:		
Weak	Mild	Strong
What church do you go to? →		
What kind of attachment do you have to your church? Check Below:		
Weak	Mild	Strong
What church do you guys plan to go to when married? →		
How do you both plan to serve and give to this church?		
If married what church do you guys go to? →		
How do you both plan to serve and give to this church?		

Systems to build our love.

22. As a family, what systems will we implement and follow to ensure we continue to build our love? Corp
23. As a family, what systems will we implement to build our individual and connected relationship with God? Corp

This question is important for all relationships engaged and abroad because no one has mastered love because love is so vast. A family that is intentional about building their love will stay in love!

So many people stop pursuing their significant other the day after their wedding or the day after they made the relationship official. Any relationship that fails to plan, plans to fail. Systems sustain. Every successful company and individual are not successful on accident they are successful on purpose. They pay attention to details, and they have systems in place to ensure their strengths become stronger, and their weaknesses become strengths. What could you both implement now to ensure you guys grow deeper in love with God and with each other?

Our Love Plan.

Take some time to think through you guys love languages and think about how you can be intentional in building your love for each other but remember none of this can happen without first developing a plan for you both to build your love in God. When you know love as a noun, you will be able to love as a verb. Navigate through the questions below and develop your plan and if you are single focus on how you plan to build your love for God and your love for yourself... without these areas being solid you will be the torpedo that sinks your future relationship.

What are your strengths?	What are your weaknesses?
What are their strengths?	What are their weakness?

In what areas do you both need to make improvements to improve the relationship?	
You:	Them:

How do you plan to deepen your relationship with God independently and collectively with your significant other?	
Independently:	Collectively:

In what ways could you love them better:	In what ways would you like to be loved better?

Our Love Accountability Tracker: Is our love increasing?

List below the things you plan to do to increase your love for God and for your significant other both independently and collectively and within the weekly tracker below write the number of the things you did each day to signify you did them. Utilize the larger box to reflect on whether or not the love is increasing in both relationships. *SO = Significant Other

On a scale, 1-10 how is your relationship with God?	
Where would you like to see it one month from now?	
On a scale, 1-10 how is your relationship with your SO?	
Where would you like to see it one month from now?	

Love Increasers:	
Independently	Collectively w/ your significant other
1	8
2	9
3	10
4	11
5	12
6	13
7	14

Week One: Goals →

Monday	Tuesday	Wednesday	Thursday	Weekend

Weekly Reflection:

Week Two: Goals →

Monday	Tuesday	Wednesday	Thursday	Weekend

Weekly Reflection:				
Week Three: Goals →				
Monday	Tuesday	Wednesday	Thursday	Weekend
Weekly Reflection:				
Week Four: Goals →				
Monday	Tuesday	Wednesday	Thursday	Weekend

Month Reflection: Wins and Lessons

$$$

24. As a family how will we handle our finances? Corp

The top two things that sink relationships are finances and infidelity. Having a solid understanding of finances and faithfulness and a plan to sustain them will help you years down the road. Utilize budgeting resources and seek to rid out any habits that are corroding your ability to steward your money. God never adds to a poor steward. Develop your systems below!

Your $tewardship Level →	Poor	So-so	Good	Great
Their $tewardship Level →	Poor	So-so	Good	Great
What do you spend the most money on?		What do they spend the most money on?		

What are you guys financial goals?
1
2
3
4
5
6
7
8
9
10
What must you cut out of your spending to reach these Goals

Financial Strategy for the next 365 days:
Today's date _____   One Year from today's date _____

Location, Location, Location!

25. As a family, what city will we live in? Cement, Corp

Key question because knowing where a person wants to live will reveal to you if you guys need to be together. Many people settle outside of the will of God due to companionship and live in a place God never intended for them to live. Being upfront and clear about where you guys will be planted is key and always remain mindful that the safest and the most profitable place is in the will of God.

What city do you want to live in →	
What city do they want to live in →	
What city do you feel God wants you both to be planted in and why?	

26. As a family, how will we communicate our concerns or fears? Cement, Corp

Without proper communication, relationships fail. The enemy destroys relationships through silence and harbored resentments. Communication is critical because without it there is no clarity. Where there is no clarity, there is confusion, and where there is confusion, there is chaos. How many families could have been saved today if someone would have humbled themselves and communicated? Little fires have burned down entire buildings, and little quarrels and harbored resentments have destroyed many relationships. The conception of every chaotic situation is the lack of communication. Now do not get me wrong not all communication is good communication there is a big difference between poor and proper communication. Communicating through arrogance and anger is poor communication but communicating through hollowness and humility is proper communication. Whenever a person communicates from a place where they feel like they know it all or at their peak of anger, they will increase the flames and the offense in the heart of the other person. However, when a person communicates from hollowness meaning being empty of resentment or offence and when they communicate through humility, they have a greater chance of putting out any potential flames.

You cannot always control the spirit of another person but you can control yours, and that begins with daily communicating with God and with yourself. When I am always communicating with God and opened to hear from him throughout my day, I can be more self-aware, and when I am more aware of myself and the will of God in each moment, I am then able to avoid confrontation or assist in diluting it if I enter one. This is key for all relationships you have to know how to recognize potential confrontation or offense, recognize when to remove yourself to calm down and when to re-engage in love and understanding. Hidden fears and concerns build over time, and what was once a molehill turns into a mountain, and what was once a seed of resentment turns into a stronghold holding your relationship back.

How is your communication? →	Poor	Decent	Solid
How could it improve?			

How is their communication? →	Poor	Decent	Solid
How could it improve?			

What areas in your relationship is chaotic now due to poor communication?

How could you improve your communication in these areas

What areas do you find it hard to communicate and why?	What areas do they find it hard to communicate and why?

How will you both keep the lines of communication open in your relationship?

We Will:

Pet Peeves!

27. What are your pet peeves and how will they affect our relationship or marriage? Cement, Corp

Everyone is annoyed by something and knowing what annoys you, and your significant other is key to developing your relationship. I believe in developing a pet peeve plan because it will help you plan on how to accommodate what annoys them and you. Now not all annoyances should be allowed we all should endeavor to grow and mature, but there are some things that do annoy us that are appropriate like the lack of attention to cleanliness, poor budgeting or any other thing that can cause internal fires. Some annoyance is petty and are due to the lack of understanding, empathy or patience. Educating yourself and seeking the why can help you be patient with your significant, others habits that are centered culturally or due to their current mature lever and will help you see where you can help them. A lot of people go into marriage culture shocked because a lot of the habits you discover post "I do" were hidden pre "I do", and a lot of what annoys you is brought up once you guys live together. That is why I always advise couples to ask each other what their proper pet peeves are so they can prepare to accommodate them so when married they will be able to avoid unnecessary conflicts.

Pet Peeve Prevention Plan:

What are your proper pet peeves and why?	What are your petty pet peeves and why?

What are their proper pet peeves and why?	What are their petty pet peeves and why?

How do you guys plan to accommodate each other's pet peeves?

What do you want your marriage to be known for?

28. What culture would we like to have in our home and abroad? Corp
29. What would we want our marriage to be known for? Cement, Corp

Legacy, legacy, legacy! What do you guys want to be known for? What do you want to be the first thought people have when they see your relationship? These answers boil down to the culture you have at home. The culture at home should be godly, pure, open, fun and full of laughter. It should be full of gentleness humility and correction. It should be a place where God is welcomed and where he inhabits but none of this is possible without being intentional. Your reputation in the streets is a reflection of your culture at home. What will be the character of your marriage and what will be its culture? Once you define these things, you will see how favored your marriage will be. Now do not forget that authenticity is key. Many couples fake their love in public but are at odds constantly at home. That is not the way to live. Develop your culture plan below and if you are single define what kind of culture you aim to have.

What do you want your marriage to be known for?		
List below the character traits you would like in your home and beside each one write yes if you match it and no if you do not. The same for your SO.		
Character Traits	Does your character match?	Does their character match?
1		
2		
3		
4		
5		
6		
7		
8		

What do you need to do to ensure this character is in your home?

Any Concerns?

    30. Is there anything I need to know that you haven't told me? Cement, Corp

    31. Are there any concerns you have about marriage? Cement, Corp

Honesty will always be the best policy. In most cases, a hard truth saves more relationships than a hidden lie discovered. It is always better, to tell the truth even at the risk of losing someone than to lie to keep them. I always tell people if you have any deep-rooted issues that you have yet to be completely delivered from with fruit to validate, then its best to stay single. Never invite people into your dysfunction because you will just end up leading them into undeserved pain. These questions are important because it will reveal how truthful they are and how they truly feel about marriage. Now do not be that kind of person that wants the truth but cannot handle the truth. Now some truths are hard to handle but make sure, before you ask, you prepare yourself to hear something that may hurt you and if you are asked this question be completely honest because everyone deserves the truth.

Marriage is supposed to be an honest place and the path to it is supposed to be an honest path. Asking if they have any concerns is wise because you do not want to find out whether they have concerns post I do.

What have they yet to tell you?	What have you yet to tell them?

What are their concerns about marriage?	What are your concerns about marriage?

Do you feel rushed?

    32. Do you feel rushed at all? Cement, Corp

Pace is important when it comes to relationships and not everyone is genuinely as ready as they think they are. Every relationship must have an environment that allows you both people to voice whether things are moving too fast or not. All relationships from God are on a timeline and God uses every nuance and situation to offer his pace, but it requires us to cooperate and to be so in tune with him that we can discern his pace and his timing. Realistically though not everyone is ready when they would like to be and it takes, maturity and wisdom to ask each other are we truly able to do this correctly financially and faithfully unto God and unto each other. It's crazy how many people hop into marriage without the ability to maintain it. People do not break the standards of marriages - the standards of marriage breaks people. It is not the position at a job that breaks people it is the responsibilities that do. Marriage is for mature adults only and maturity is only found in fellowshipping with God. Do not rush the process. It doesn't matter how fast everyone else is going because divorce is high for a reason. Whatever you rush into you will ruin. Pace yourself; His timing is perfect.

Do they feel rushed at all if so why?	Do you feel rushed at all if so why?

Noticed anything?

33. How do you honestly view me this far in our relationship? Cement, Corp
34. So far in the relationship have you noticed anything I need to improve on? Cement, Corp

This question is one of my favorites because it reveals a person's desire to grow and it opens up the opportunity for you to see the health of the relationship. Check-ins are important! It is good to check in with your significant other to see how happy they are. I heard Tim Keller say that marriage is two people flowing in and out of love but staying together. The reality is you may always love them but you will not always like them or be in love with them, and it is important to humbly ask how you are performing in the relationship, where you need to improve and how they view you.

Catching a person off guard can sometimes give you the best answers, not necessary through their words, but through their body language. You need to know how they genuinely view you and what their plans are for you. Check their body language, tone and most importantly their actions because talk is cheap and actions are expensive, and people are quick to purchase words but do not have enough to pay for it through their actions. If you hear it, more than you see it; leave it.

How do they view you so far?	How do you view them this far?

In what areas did they say you needed to improve?

Love Languages.

35. What's your love language? Or how do you like to receive love? Cement, Corp

Knowing each other's love language is important because it will help you best serve your partner and how best you like to be served. There are 5 Love Languages, and they are found if Gary Chapmans book the 5 Love Languages and they are

- Words of Affirmation
- Acts of Service
- Receiving Gifts
- Quality Time and
- Physical Touch.

Head over to 5lovelanguages.com to take their free assessment and see what each other's love languages are. And never forget selfless love is the best kind of love.

What are your love languages?	What are their love languages?

What are your views on sex in a relationship?

36. What are your views on sex in a relationship? Cloud, Cement

This is a very important question, and it needs to be asked early on in the cement stage if not the cloud stage of the relationship. Lust is a very dangerous cancer and when it latches onto a person; its effects on them in a relationship are so dangerous because lust is never satisfied. No one is capable of appeasing lust and knowing a person's lust level is important because no matter how mild it is it will desire sex or other sexual activity.

Many marriages have been contaminated by lust since day one due to undealt with issues like pornography and addictions to sex of all kinds. What a person practices will manifest itself in a relationship. Purity is important, and waiting is key because many people who struggle with lust only linger for the sex and don't really want you as a person. Take the time to hear their answers but also observe their actions to see how committed they are to waiting until marriage. As you have heard me say before, sex is only safe in a marriage where both the husband and wife are completely submitted to God nowhere else is sex safe. Sex is not safe single or safe in a marriage with only one-person committed to God. A person's level of commitment to God will determine their commitment to you. Their purity of heart towards God will determine their purity of hearts towards you and away from you.

What is their commitment level to God?			
Commitment Level →	Poor	So-so	Great
What is your commitment level to God?			
Commitment Level →	Poor	So-so	Great

What are their views on sex before marriage?		
Do their actions match their views? →	Yes	No
What are your views on sex before marriage?		
Do your actions match your views? →	Yes	No

What is supporting your relationship?

    37. Where will we anchor our roots as a family? Cement, Corp

Roots are important to every tree, especially to a family tree. Roots reach for support. Their goal is to reach for resources and to reach for rocks to help secure the tree's goal in bearing fruit. Where does your family reach for support? Those supports can be in leisure, relaxation, spiritual support, emotional stability, fun, creativity etc. Wherever you and your mate find support both individually or collectively matters and they need to be defined and allowed. Roots are important but what they are reaching for are even more important! Make sure what you as an individual or as a family are reaching towards matches your families goals, desired outcomes and that they truly support you all growing closer to God and close to one another.

What are the main things your relationship is rooted in now?
1
2
3
4
5
6
7

What do you value most out of a relationship or marriage?		
Are the values listed above still valued in your relationship? →	Yes	No
If single, are they being prepared for? →	Yes	No
What are your relationship goals and/or desired outcomes?		

How is your overall health? →	Poor	Decent	Excellent
How is your overall health helping or hurting your relationship?			
How is their overall health? →	Poor	Decent	Excellent
How is their overall health helping or hurting the relationship?			
How healthy is your relationship overall? →	Poor	Decent	Excellent

What habits in your relationship could be causing your roots to rot.

What do you both do creatively and for fun; individually and collectively?

Individually	Collectively

How often do you do these things? → | Rarely | Sometimes | often

How could doing these things more often strengthen your relationship?

How committed is your relationship to the things of God?

Prayer:

How often do you pray →	Rarely	Sometimes	Often	Everyday
How often do they pray →	Rarely	Sometimes	Often	Everyday
How often do ya'll pray together? →	Rarely	Sometimes	Often	Everyday

If every day is not circled write down below what is hindering prayer in your relationship.

Reading the Bible:

How often do you read →	Rarely	Sometimes	Often	Everyday
How often do they read →	Rarely	Sometimes	Often	Everyday
How often do ya'll read together? →	Rarely	Sometimes	Often	Everyday

If every day is not circled, write down below what is hindering you guys from reading your bibles.

Obedience

How often do you listen and obey →	Rarely	Sometimes	Often	Everyday
How often do they listen and obey →	Rarely	Sometimes	Often	Everyday
How often do ya'll seek and obey →	Rarely	Sometimes	Often	Everyday

If often and every day is not circled, write down below what is hindering you guys from making out time to seek and obey God.

Habits and Hobbies

We are all creatures of habits. We are what we habitually do. Habits can either help or hinder a relationship, and it's important for you to see not only their good and bad habits but yours as well!

38. What hobbies can we share in our marriage? Corp
39. What are your favorite hobbies to do alone and why? Cloud, Cement
40. What are your favorite hobbies to do with others and why? Cloud, Cement
41. How can we have a balance in our marriage when it comes to the hobbies we love to do alone or with friends? Corp
42. How often would you like to do things on your own and with me? Cement, Corp

A relationship is two individuals sharing a bond with the goal of reaching the same destination. The key word in that sentence is individuals. A relationship that robs you of your individuality is not a relation(ship) to be on. You have to have time together and time apart because trust me it is the time apart that makes a person long for your love more so than always being around you. It is important to have healthy hobbies together and apart but make sure they are healthy and helpful hobbies not hurtful helpless ones. Some hobbies hurt people individually and hurt couples collectively. Purity and discipline is key to ensure this does not happen. Your hobbies must be pure, and they should aid discipline not corrode it. Make sure to ask why and observe their body language and really seek to find out what they love to do alone and with you and if they do have things they love to do alone let them do it and support it especially if they do it in a balanced and pure way.

What are their favorite hobbies to do with you and to do alone?	
With you	Alone
1	
2	
3	
4	

Why these things with you?	Why these things Alone?

What are your favorite hobbies to do with them and to do alone?	
With them	Alone
1	
2	
3	
4	
Why these things with them?	Why these things Alone?

How often do you each of you need to do each hobby and are they balanced?			
How often do they need to do hobby #1 alone		Days a week:	
How balanced are they →	Really Balanced	Not Balanced	Helps Relationship	Hurts Relationship.
How often do they need to do hobby #2 alone		Days a week:	
How balanced are they →	Really Balanced	Not Balanced	Helps Relationship	Hurts Relationship.
How often do they need to do hobby #3 alone		Days a week:	
How balanced are they →	Really Balanced	Not Balanced	Helps Relationship	Hurts Relationship.
How often do they need to do hobby #4 alone		Days a week:	
How balanced are they →	Really Balanced	Not Balanced	Helps Relationship	Hurts Relationship.
Areas to improve:			
How often do they need to do hobby #1 alone		Days a week:	
How balanced are they →	Really Balanced	Not Balanced	Helps Relationship	Hurts Relationship.
How often do they need to do hobby #2 alone		Days a week:	
How balanced are they →	Really Balanced	Not Balanced	Helps Relationship	Hurts Relationship.
How often do they need to do hobby #3 alone		Days a week:	

How balanced are they →	Really Balanced	Not Balanced	Helps Relationship	Hurts Relationship.
How often do they need to do hobby #4 alone			Days a week:	
How balanced are they →	Really Balanced	Not Balanced	Helps Relationship	Hurts Relationship.
Areas to improve:				

Celebrating Accomplishments

43. What do you like to do to celebrate accomplishments etc.? Cloud

Accomplishing goals are exciting and knowing what they like to do to celebrate small or big accomplishments can help add joy and fire to the relationship. Remember, if God is in what they do; when they win you win!

What do they like to do to celebrate small accomplishments?	What do they like to do to celebrate big accomplishments
What do you like to do to celebrate small accomplishments?	What do you like to do to celebrate big accomplishments

Emotional Reactions

44. Where do you go to first when you experience a disappointment? Cloud, Cement, Corp
45. When sad what do you do? Cloud, Cement, Corp
46. When happy what do you do? Cloud, Cement, Corp

Where a person goes when they are extremely happy or sad tells a lot about where they find their hope. For a while, food was the first thing I went to when I was disappointed. I would rush to a 7/11 or Bojangles to try to make myself feel happy, but that place only aided in me gaining weight… even though it took my pain away temporary it left me with unwanted weight. Now I embrace the joy and the fewer calories that comes when I go to God **first**. He is the only one that can truly help me or you cope with disappointments, but we have to always remember that sadness is temporary and joy is eternal and keeping our trust in him is the only way our relationships will stay afloat even in turbulent weather.

Carve out some time to process this question by yourself and with your significant other because the first door we should bang on when disappointed is God's door!

Also:

Knowing where they use to go to could give you a hint of where they go now or may go in the future when tested. Like I always advise, do not marry a person whom you have yet to see how they handle success and disappointments. Sometimes a person responds poorly when on top than when they are low. Take the time to see how they handle their highs and lows. Lastly, a positive place without God is not a positive place meaning some people have "happy places" to escape their problems, but they do not seek God there. Make sure that where they go and where you go to detox; God is the one you are meeting there.

Do you struggle with depression? →	Yes	No
Do they struggle with depression?	Yes	No
From observation, what do they do when sad or upset?		
What positive or negative places do they go to or use to go to when disappointed?		

Are they meeting God there? →	Yes	No	Not sure.
What positive or negative places do you go to or use to go to when disappointed?			
Are you meeting God there? →	Yes	No	

Fun but important questions to get to know your potential mate or your current spouse. You may already know the answers but make sure you find out anyway.

47. What is their favorite restaurant and why? Cloud, Cement
48. What is your favorite restaurant and why? Cloud, Cement

Their favorite restaurant and why?
Your favorite restaurant and why?

49. What is their favorite snack and why? Cloud, Cement
50. What is your favorite snack and why? Cloud, Cement

Their favorite snack and why?
Your favorite snack and why?

51. What is their favorite dessert and why? Cloud, Cement
52. What is your favorite dessert and why? Cloud, Cement

Their favorite dessert and why?

Your favorite dessert and why?

53. What is their favorite TV show and why? Cloud, cement
54. What is your favorite TV show and why? Cloud, cement

Their favorite TV show and why?

Your favorite TV show and why?

55. What is their favorite magazines or books? Cloud, Cement, corp.
56. What is your favorite magazines or books? Cloud, Cement, corp.

Their favorite magazines and why?

Your favorite magazines and why?

57. What foods do they not like and why? Cloud, cement
58. What foods do you not like and why? Cloud, cement

Foods they don't like and why?

Foods you don't like and why?

More money more problems solved.

    59. If money wasn't an issue, what would you pursue or produce? Cloud, Cement, Corp

Fun question to ask and to use to dream together. It is also a good question to hear what they really would like to do if money was not an option.

What would they do if money wasn't an option?

What would you do if money weren't an option?

What would you both do together if money weren't an option?

Deal Breakers!

60. Are there any hobbies or habits that are deal breakers for you? Cloud, Cement, Corp

Deal or no deal is the question. Not everyone is designed and equipped to be with everyone and that's ok. Some people have hobbies that are for whatever reason going to be in their lives until they are dead and it is ok to walk away from them. You have to know what you will or will not accept or what will be too uncomfortable for you to live around. This does not mean that you nick pick but it does mean that you establish healthy guidelines for yourself and not cross them for any reason or for anyone.

What are their deal breakers?		
Deal or no deal for you?	Deal	No Deal
What are your deal breakers?		
Deal or no deal for them?	Deal	No Deal

Do I annoy you?

61. Since we have been in a relationship, have you noticed any bad/ good habits from me? Cement, Corp
62. What do I regularly do that annoys you and why? Cement, Corp
63. What hobbies do I do that affect you in a bad way and why? Cement, Corp

Good check in questions to see where you can improve or have improved. Creating a culture of growth is important in any relationship. Both you and your partner should have a free and clear airspace to fly these kinds of questions through because if you grow, it helps them and if they grow, it helps you. The real test though is finding someone who welcomes this kind of culture. We all have areas to improve and having someone who loves you to ask you these questions and having someone that you love to ask them to is essential for growth. We all annoy each other sometimes, but people who constantly grow find ways to minimize them.

What do you do to annoy them?
1
2
3
4
In what ways can you improve in these areas?

What do they do to annoy you?
1
2
3
4
In what ways are they willing to improve in these areas?

Good and Bad habits

64. What are your bad habits? Cloud, Cement, Corp
65. What are your good habits? Cloud, cement, Corp

Not everyone, in the beginning, is going to be willing to share their bad habits with you especially when they are trying to WOO you but utilize the two things that cannot lie, and those are your eyes. The eye test with godly discernment is the best test. Take time to observe and log in their good habits below and the bad habits you may have noticed.

What are their good habits?	
1	
2	
3	
4	
5	
What are their bad habits?	
Habits	Deal Breaker? Yes or No
1	
2	
3	
4	
5	

66. Do you struggle with any sexual habits if so what and how are you fixing it? Cement, Corp

You must know the answer to this question. This question is definitely for the cement and corporation stages of the relationship because as I said earlier lust has no boundaries like love. Lust blinds people causing them to think that their private sexual habits are not a danger to their marriage, but they are. Hidden or known sexual habits will be used against you, your mate and your relationship at large. Sexual habits were designed to be shared between a husband and a wife and not with anything or anyone outside of that union. If they come clean and answer honestly but are nonchalant about it and unwilling to change then you should seek to exit the relationship.

You can't help them or save them only God can. Anyone who struggles with a sexual sin must deal with them outside of a relationship due to the dangerous effects of them. If you are married, pray that God will open their hearts to council so that your marriage can progress!

What sexual habits do they struggle with?		
Are they seeking help? →	Yes	No
Who are they seeking help from? →		
What sexual habits do you struggle with?		
Are you seeking help? →	Yes	No
Who are you seeking help from? →		

Addictions

    67. Do you struggle with any addictions if so what and how are you fixing it? Cloud, Cement, Corp

One of the top silent killers of relationships are addictions. An addiction is an excessive connection or dependence on a person, product, place or perspective. These four areas are where many people struggle with addictions. Let us start with people. A person can be excessively attached to a person through a mild or major soul tie. These soul ties are birth through deep infatuations or deep longings for companionship. This kind of addiction is birth out of **need**. Need leads to perversion. When a person desperately needs someone, they will be addicted or consumed with everything they do. Next, let us look at the main one products. This is the area where you will find most people addicted, but the thing about products likes, drugs, social media, pornography, sex, food, etc. is that they are used to mask a deeper void, which is a person's depravity and deep need for God. When a person is not connected to God properly, through salvation and being surgically operated through the sanctification process, then they will begin to engage in situations that will cause that void to deepen leading them to products to help them escape temporarily. Due to ignorance and pride, people will always seek a temporary fix over an eternal one. God is the only one that can fill our voids but until we realize that, our depraved hearts will always aim to reach to what is close to us. Any product or person that is closest to us during this phase of our lives we will reach for.

Let us now look at places and perspectives. Many people may not recognize these as addictions, but they are. Places become addictive when we idolize the peace of that place meaning the need to always go there to hide or mask our deep wounds. These places can be strip clubs, a boyfriend or girlfriends house, a restaurant, etc. any place where we cannot stop going to or that we seek to be our sole source of renewal can be an addiction. Last but not least perspectives. Some people are overly connected to an idea, a movement or worldview to the point that even if the convincing truth is present, they will still hold on to their views. Many people are attached to perspectives or ideas due to them finding their worth and value in them. They make them feel significant. It's crazy how many people find their significance in lies? It is our responsibility to find the truth behind every matter and once we find the truth assess the resistance to that truth. Every truth has the power to set you free. It is important for you to understand your addictions and your significant others addictions so that you can see how they affect your relationship or your marriage. Anything, anyone, any place or any perspective that you cannot go long periods without it is an addiction.

The devil wants us addicted because he knows that addictions can be in your life forever even post salvation. He knows the effects of emotional wounds he knows that emotional needs will lead to emotional connections, emotional connections will lead to potential emotional wounds, and emotional wounds without emotional maturity will lead to emotional addictions or cycles. This question is a layered one and is serious; take some time below to access your addictions and your significant other addictions and develop a plan to overcome them. Also, remember the only way to overcome ad addiction is through the following

- self-**awareness** (knowing yourself and seeing how these addictions are destroying your life),
- **ask** God for help and repent for your carnal attachments,
- **attach** yourself to him and allow him to renew you; disassociating yourself completely from the addiction,
- **assist** God in his mission for your life and constantly be productive and
- **act/** be intentional in fulfilling the work of God.

For more info on this topic, please check out my book the Purpose of Freedom.

What addictions do they struggle with?			
Are they seeking help? →		Yes	No
Who are they seeking help from? →			
What addictions do you struggle with?			
Are you seeking help? →		Yes	No
Who are you seeking help from? →			

Godly Habits

68. What are some habits that you do to strengthen your relationship with God? Cloud, Cement, Corp
69. What are some new habits we can implement into our relationship to keep us growing in God? Cement, Corp

We are only as strong as our spiritual disciplines. Too many people are flashy but are not sound fundamentally. They look spiritually strong online but are spiritually weak in person. God can careless about how you look online he audits how you live offline. Every day it is important for us to build ourselves in our most holy faith. Each of us were dealt a measure of faith to work and to build on. So many of us have yet to do anything with our measure of faith and we wonder why we are not progressing. Every day you must be intentional in developing your faith because whether you like it or not life will test it. A relationship that doesn't grow in the things of God will eventually fail. What are you and your significant other doing daily to grow in the things of God? What do you do individually and collectively to ensure the faith and the foundation of your family is strong? Good habits are nothing without godly habits to support them!

What are you going to do to strengthen your relationship with God?	How often?
1	
2	
3	
4	
5	

Place the number of the habit above on the day you performed that habit and let's see if you can strengthen this habit in 21 days! Remember this page number so you can utilize this tracker.

D1	D2	D3
D4	D5	D6
D7	D8	D9
D10	D11	D12
D15	D14	D15
D16	D17	D18
D19	D20	D21
Godly Habit #1 →	Sunk below	Stayed the same	Got stronger
Godly Habit #2 →	Sunk below	Stayed the same	Got stronger
Godly Habit #3 →	Sunk below	Stayed the same	Got stronger
Godly Habit #4 →	Sunk below	Stayed the same	Got stronger
Godly Habit #5 →	Sunk below	Stayed the same	Got stronger

What are they doing to strengthen their relationship with God?	How often?
1	
2	
3	
4	
5	

What are you both doing together to strengthen your marriages connection to God?	How often?
1	
2	
3	
4	

5	

When will be our date nights?

70. When will be our date nights? Cement, Corp

Being in a committed relationship and being married requires both individuals to be intentional even when they don't feel like it. Marriage is not a sprint it is a marathon, and there are certain stretches that are going to feel long but you have to be intentional, and that intentionality must come from intimacy with God. God is the huge power source that desires to be connected to all marriages. He knows the weight two imperfect people will have to carry during certain stages in life, and he knows that it is going to take something beyond their physical ability to help supply what each other needs. That is why we must have a thriving; intimate relationship with God so that we can do what feels hard to do at times.

One of the things couples will need to be intentional about is setting date nights. Creating new moments even during tough times and being intentional in dressing up and reliving fun moments is important. Removing yourself temporarily from the heaviness of life and getting back to the roots of why you both grew in love in the first place will help your relationship tremendously. Carve out some consistent time to go out and ask some rekindling questions to keep the flame burning.

How connected are you with God?	Connected	Not connected as I should
How is your connection or the lack thereof to God affecting the flame of your relationship?		
How connected are they to God?	Connected	Not connected as they should
How is their connection or the lack thereof to God affecting the flame of your relationship?		
Your top dating places or ideas	Their top dating places or ideas.	

1	1
2	2
3	3
4	4
5	5
6	6
7	7
8	8
9	9
10	10
How often would you like to go on dates in a month? →	
How often would they like to go on dates in a month? →	
Final: When are date nights? →	
What is the first date night activity since doing this exercise →	

Sports

71. Did you play sports growing up if so which ones? Cloud

Cool question to ask and if they didn't play any sports; ask them what did they like to do growing up and why?

What sports did they play or →	Other activities
1	1
2	2
3	3
4	4
What sports did you play or →	Other activities
1	1
2	2
3	3
4	4

Stumbling?

72. Do I in any way cause you to stumble into any bad habits? Cement, Corp

Very important question to ask. We are at times the reflection of what we allow other people to do, and sometimes we allow our love for them to silence us but in return hurt ourselves. For example sexual sins. Sometimes women or men will silence their purity for the sake of having someone and will practice sexual sins to keep them. Some people will silence their views on music or eating for the sake of having someone, and they will fall into bad habits that they were once strong in. Either way, silence is never the answer, and you both need to be vocal about what the other person is doing to cause you to stumble. Never forget their answer and or their actions after you have told them will reveal to you their intentions with you.

If applicable:

What are they doing to cause you to stumble?
What did they say you do to cause them to stumble?

Stressors

73. What do you do to cope with stress? Cloud, Cement, Corp

Stress is a killer, and it has killed off many people throughout history. Some studies even say that stress is the leading cause or the conceptual cause of most deaths. If this is true which I believe it is then it is important that you guys discuss stress. How a person handles stress will determine the stress they add to others. No stress should be eternalized it should be funneled out through healthy and pure habits that will channel that stress out of your mind and body. Stress is a silent killer. It weakens you overtime and will ruin your relationships. Take the time to really discuss with your partner the importance of establishing healthy habits that will keep you and your family stress-free.

What is stressing them and how are they handling their stress?	
Stressors	Stress relievers
1	1
2	2
3	3
4	4
What conceived their stressors above:	
Stressor #1	
Stressor #2	
Stressor #3	
Stressor #4	
What is stressing you and how are you handling your stress?	
Stressors	Stress relievers
1	1
2	2
3	3
4	4
What conceived your stressors above:	
Stressor #1	
Stressor #2	
Stressor #3	
Stressor #4	

How can you ensure your potential marriage or marriage is stress-free?

Health

74. Do you like to work out? If so/not why? Cloud, Cement, Corp
75. What did you eat today/ week? Cloud, Cement, Corp
76. What are your daily rituals? Cloud, Cement, Corp

Marriage is an investment, and before anyone invests in it, they have to ensure that the person they are investing in the marriage with is healthy as well. So many people take their time and youth for granted. Many people in their 20's and 30's overlook their health thinking they will always feel good. Bad things can still grow in a body that "feels" good. It is important for you to see healthy habits practiced in the one you want to marry or are married too because a healthy marriage is only as healthy as the people involved. Now if you are in a relationship with someone and they have failed in their health one of the best ways to inspire them is through action. No one wants to see their wife or husband workout alone in an environment with other fit people. Utilize this method to lure them into shape. For those that are single or dating make sure you take your health and the health of your prospect seriously. Having workout dates could stimulate your relationship. Set up workout dates where you guys can take classes or lift together and go to a smoothie shop or a healthy restaurant to ask questions from the dating prep game. →

How's their health? →	Failing	Poor	So-so	Excellent	Not Sure
What is causing their health to be poor?					

Are they willing to work on their health →	Yes	No
How could you support them in becoming healthy?		

How's your health? →	Failing	Poor	So-so	Excellent	Not Sure
What is causing your health to be poor?					

Are you willing to work on their health →	Yes	No
How would you like your significant other to support you in becoming healthy?		

Healthy Habits: what healthy habits did you guys decide to incorporate in your relationship and how often?

Habits	How often
1	
2	
3	
4	
5	

Place the number of the habit above on the day you performed that habit and let's see if you can strengthen this habit in 21 days! Remember this page number so you can utilize this tracker.

D1	D2	D3
D4	D5	D6
D7	D8	D9
D10	D11	D12

D15	D14	D15	
D16	D17	D18	
D19	D20	D21	
Godly Habit #1 →	Sunk below	Stayed the same	Got stronger
Godly Habit #2 →	Sunk below	Stayed the same	Got stronger
Godly Habit #3 →	Sunk below	Stayed the same	Got stronger
Godly Habit #4 →	Sunk below	Stayed the same	Got stronger
Godly Habit #5 →	Sunk below	Stayed the same	Got stronger
Reflection:			

THEO

77. What do you believe in spiritually?

This question is by far one of the most important questions to ask because what a person believes spiritually will determine what they will feel emotionally and pursue physically. Knowing what a person believes when it comes to God is extremely important and it may take some real thorough observation to see what they truly believe. See many people believe in the person of God but how many of them believe in faith the plan, principles, and promises of God? Only trials and temptations will truly reveal what they truly believe. For this section of questions, discernment is key because not everyone will tell the truth. Many people when they hear the term unequally yoked they go straight to the idea of being unequally yoked with a non-believer which in context is true, but there is a thing of being unequally yoked with a person spiritually. Not every believer is on the same level, and you must make sure you trust God to match you with a person that is progressive spiritually within the confines of scripture of course and desires God more than you.

What do they believe in spiritually?			
How's their fruit so far →	Removed or non-existent	Rotten	Ripe
What do you believe in spiritually?			
How's your fruit so far →	Removed or non-existent	Rotten	Ripe

Is Jesus God?

78. Do you believe that Jesus is God? Cloud, Cement, Corp

Believing in God is cool but when you give that God the name Jesus things get interesting. There is power in names, and there is power in the perception of a name. When you have a name, and you have adopted lies about who you are, suddenly, your name lacks value and meaning to you but when you accept who you are in Christ your name will have immense value and power. The thing though with the name of Jesus is that it has power, but a person's perception of his name will hinder that power working for them. Culture doesn't have a problem with the term God because anyone with common sense can recognize the divine design within creation but people fall back when you say Jesus is God. See the Godhead is comprised of three unique but in harmony individuals

1. God the Father
2. God the Son and
3. God the Holy Ghost

God is three in one like we are;

1. We are a spirit
2. We have a soul and
3. We live in a body

Man in the Garden of Eden was in harmony like God until the woman engaged in a conversation with the fallen angel Satan. Satan tricked the woman into eating from the forbidden tree who then passed the fruit to Adam who was with her and he ate. At this moment their eyes were opened and they recognize that they were naked. When God recognized their altered self-awareness he separated them from Eden or in other words his presence. But in order for God to be reconciled back to man there had to be a payment. This payment had a God price tag on it meaning only God could pay the debt. So God before he even created woman created her womb to not allow her blood to mix with her baby's blood creating a door for God to enter as a man. He chose a woman by the name of Mary to house the physical expression of himself and through the Holy Spirit planted a holy seed that would open the door for Christ, God's anointed to be conceived. His spirit was Christ his flesh was Jesus making him able to function and feel this realm. See God as a spirit couldn't feel what we felt so he had to enter our world so that he could pay the price of our sins and establish a connection once again with us. Jesus is the physical expression of the father and is equal to him and his spirit the Holy Spirit is Jesus spirt dwelling within those who believe.

Make sure you study your faith for yourself so that you can be able to stand strong and not waiver.

Do they believe that Jesus is God? →	Yes	No
Why or why not?		

After doing research what did you learn about the divinity of Jesus?

79. How's your relationship with God? Cloud, Cement, Corp

This question is a question that can be asked at any stage of your relationship because walking with God is not an easy journey and there will be ups and downs. The true test is during bad times. Observing how a person reacts towards God and their response time when mad at God will let you know the state of their relationship with God. There is nothing wrong with being upset/ frustrated with God while maturing, but there is something wrong if that person up and leaves him. It's hard to leave someone you truly love. Take some time to listen and observe how they respond to God's ways and see what ways of theirs comes to the surface.

Also, make sure you observe how they are with you because a person who is not committed to God will not be committed to you. Talk is cheap, and many people boast of having a relationship with God, but the real question is what kind? You want to be with someone that honors God and you can't have honor without love. Jesus said if you love me you will KEEP my commandments. You can't keep without love. If you desire to be kept, make sure they deeply love God.

How's their relationship with God?	Non-existent	Poor	So-so	Thriving
How's your relationship with God?	Non-existent	Poor	So-so	Thriving
Observations of their commitment to God:				
Month one:				
Month two				
Month three				

Church Hurt

80. Have you experienced any church hurt if so how does that affect your relationship with God and going to church? Cloud, cement

One of the number one reasons why people are at odds with God is due to their experiences in Church. So many people have been hurt by people who profess to know and love God and have left the faith. Some have allowed their hurts to validate their current lifestyles and decisions. God understands church hurt and will vindicate, but he will not underwrite or support how many of us react or act due to it. God is our source the church is a resource, and we must make sure we don't allow our vulnerabilities to lead us into getting hurt. See, during moments of vulnerability voids can birth and where there are voids, there are vultures. Not everyone in the church is converted, and not one person that's converted in the church is perfect. No matter where you go there will always be human error. That's why it is extremely important for you and me only to put our trust in God and only allow him to handle us when vulnerable. Vultures will always circle the wounded and a lot of vultures visit and serve churches to take advantage of the weak. This question is important and needs to be asked because you don't want to be in a situation where you guys set yourselves up to be hurt or hinder yourselves from being a part of a healthy biblical community. I did a video on YouTube called how to heal from Church Hurt that goes into greater detail feel free to watch this video alone or with your significant other and comment and let me know you are watching this video because of reading Dating Prep.

Have they experienced church hurt? →		Yes	no
If so what happened?			
Are they better or still bitter from the situation? →		Better	Bitter
Have you experienced church hurt? →		Yes	no
If so what happened?			
Are you better or still bitter from the situation? →		Better	Bitter

What must you both do to process and push through this hurt?	
You	Significant other

Prayer

81. How's your prayer life? How often do you pray? Cloud, Cement, Corp

Prayer is a powerful resource and being connected to someone that knows how to pray is important. Prayer and praise are the only two things we have here on earth that can touch heaven. You can't touch heaven with any other instrument other than prayer. Prayer is a dialogue, not a monologue. It's a conversation that is birth out of a thriving relationship with God. It is our connection to our exclusive power source.

No prayer no power know prayer know power.

You want to make sure you are connected to someone that can touch heaven on your behalf. Someone that can cover you when you can't cover yourself. Someone that can tap into heaven on your behalf. But prayers that come from a heart that doesn't honor God or a heart that is in secret sin will not touch heaven shoot; they will barely even touch their ceiling. This walk with God is not an easy one, and you must make sure you and your significant other are people of prayer tapping into heaven to ensure both of you are prayed up and supported.

How's their prayer life? →	Non-existent	Poor	Steady	Fiery
How often do they pray? →	Never	Rarely	sometimes	Daily
What is interfering with their prayer time?				

How's your prayer life? →	Non-existent	Poor	Steady	Fiery
How often do you pray? →	Never	Rarely	sometimes	Daily
What is interfering with your prayer time?				

→

Write down below things you need to cover in prayer daily and utilize this list to ensure you pray daily. Feel free to go to YouTube and type in *Joshua Eze prayer* to learn more about prayer. Remember prayer is a dialogue make sure you still yourself often to hear from God!

Prayer list	
Your needs	Your significant others needs
Your children	Other Family Members
Property + Possessions	Friends + Associates + Enemies
Leaders + Supporters	Personal Development + Growth

Ideas + Goals	Random
Other	**Other**

Praise Reports and Answered Prayers

Praise Reports and Answered Prayers	Date Answered

Questions on the Bible.

82. What are your views on the Bible? Cloud
83. How often do you read your Bible? Cloud
84. What passage from the Bible are you reading now and what are you getting from it? Cloud, Cement, Corp

Everything that was made, was made by a manufacturer and was assisted with a manual. The best way to know how to operate anything is to ask its manufacture or to check its manual. We too have a manufacturer and a manual, and that's God and the Bible, and if we have any questions about marriage, money, manhood or womanhood, we can ask God or consult his word. The world is lost today due to not consulting God or his word. If you remove God from culture, and remove the honor or the discipline to search his word then we will mismanage everything here. Your management ability reflects your closeness to the manufacture and his manual and the same goes for your significant other or prospect. Knowing their views on the bible will let you know what they stand on and before you can ask someone this question, you must have an intellectual understanding of why you know the bible to be true. Like all manuals they are perfect in explaining its products origin, how it's to be used, what happens when it's misused or when it malfunctions, how to recognize when it's not operating properly, how to redeem it and how to function it properly. The bible does the same thing; its lets us know

- Our origin, (God)
- how we were originally supposed to operate (Before the fall)
- what caused us to malfunction (Sin)
- how to recognize our imperfections (God's Grace and Our Repentance)
- How to be redeemed and how to live the original way.

It is important for you to know this for yourself so that you can be able to process their answer.

How often they read and what passage they are reading now is important too because the more you engage with something, the more that something enters you. Your actions reflect what you engage with the most, and if a person rarely prays or reads their bible, then that person will rarely act like God.

What are their views on the bible?				
How often do they read their bible? →	Never	Rarely	Often	Daily
What passage are they reading from the bible now? →				
Random Ask:				
What passage are they reading from the bible now? →				
What passage are they reading from the bible now? →				
What passage are they reading from the bible now? →				
What are your views on the bible? Or what have you learned about the inerrancy of scripture?				
How often do you read your bible? →	Never	Rarely	Often	Daily

Reading plan: If you don't already have a Bible reading plan I want you to follow the one below. There are three ways to read/ study the bible

1. Systematic
2. Specific
3. Sporadic (randomly led by the Holy Spirit)

Below I will give you a plan that encompasses all 3!

Systematic: A Gospel a month and a Proverb a Day. Reading a Gospel a month over and over and over for the whole month helps you get closer to the person of Jesus and helps you see how he handled situations. It also helps you to deeply process his teachings. Start with this month and follow this plan:

Month #1 (This Month)	Matthew
Month #2	Mark
Month #3	Luke
Month #4	John
Month #5	Acts
Month #6	Matthew again and so on

Take some time to utilize the a notebook to journal what you are learning from your readings!

A proverb a day keeps wicked schemes away. Each day look to see what day it is and simply ready that Proverb. For example if its Tuesday June 19th read Proverbs 19. Each day take one proverb from that chapter that resonated with you and write it on a notecard and meditate on it that day as well as see how you can put into action.

Specific: Specific reading is reading Gods word to help build you up in a specific area for instance if you are struggling with worry simply go to openbible.info and under the topical section type in worry and pull at lead 3 to 5 scriptures on that topic and write them either on a note card or below and meditate on those scriptures by utilizing them in prayer for instance Father I know you will supply all of my needs according to your riches and glory by Christ Jesus so I will not worry. Philippines 4:19 or by devoting time to memorize them and utilizing them when tempted in that area. Utilize the section below to help you out.

Struggle #1 →	
Scripture #1 →	
Write it out as a prayer	
Write it out 3 times for memory purposes	

1	
2	
3	

Scripture 2 →	
Write it out as a prayer	

Write it out 3 times for memory purposes
1
2
3

Scripture 3 →	
Write it out as a prayer	

Write it out 3 times for memory purposes
1
2
3

*For other struggles utilize the method above in a separate notebook.

Questions on Confirmation

85. Have you sought God about me? Cement, Corp
86. Now that things are getting somewhat serious what kind of fast do we need to go on? Cement
87. Now that we are getting serious how do you view my spiritual walk? Cement
88. In what areas could I improve in? Cement, Corp

No relationship should emerge from the friendship stage to the serious stage without confirmation from God. God must be the one that conceives your relationship because whoever conceives it will be responsible for carrying it. Before you go to the next level, you both must take some time to fast and pray and ask God to confirm it. That's why it is important to build your discernment during your offseason or when you are single so that when you are being recruited or when you need a new star player for your team you will let the Holy Spirit be the GM and select your franchise player through the draft. Seeing that discernment comes from the same area our feelings are if we catch feelings before we seek confirmation, we will confuse our feelings as confirmation. Infatuation makes any attractive situation feel right, but feelings are not factual. A person who is led dominantly by their emotions is a person who is set to fail. We must be so in love with God and trusting in his timing that when a good thing comes our way we can tell it no if it's not a God thing. The problem is not with us telling bad things, no, it is in us telling good things no. Not every good thing is a God thing, and you must be able to tell the difference. If you feel it getting serious, take some time to design a fast to seek confirmation on the relationship and when it should level up. This practice will help you, and your significant other take every major situation to God.

Also auditing each other's spiritual walk is important as well. Sometimes we can be walking with God crooked, and we need someone to help straighten our walk.

How infatuated are you? →	Extremely	Kind of a little	Eh	Not at all
What must you do to dilute your infatuation?				
How infatuated are you? →	Extremely	Kind of a little	Eh	Not at all
How long have you guys been together? →	Days	Months		Years
Has God confirmed your current relationship?			Yep	Nope

If so how did he confirm it?

If not what must you due to positions yourself to hear from God

Questions on God in the Family

89. How are we going to keep God in our relationship and marriage? Cement, Corp
90. What systems do we need to implement to ensure we grow spiritually? Cement, Corp
91. What will our devotional time look like when married? Corp
92. How will we teach our kids the things of God? Corp
93. When married how will we serve our local church together? Corp
94. What church will we go to? Corp

There is nothing more exciting in a relationship than engaging the things of God together. Incorporating God should be the number one item on any relationships agenda. Not incorporating him fully into every aspect of your relationship will set your relationship up to fail. There must be a plan for every area of your relationship now and for where you guys want to take the relationship. God must be number one in your life and your relationship, and he must be at the center of everything. He can't be on the edge or at the bottom of your top ten he must be #1 and at the center because you will feel the effects of him not being where he needs to be. What are you going to implement in your relationship to ensure God is #1 and at the center? How will your individual and collective devotional times look like meaning how will you guys engage with God separately and as a family and how will you guys serve together? A couple that serves God together grows in the things of God together.

What are the top things in your life right now and how is God in the center of each area?	
1	
2	
3	
4	
5	
6	
7	
8	
9	
10	

How are you going to keep God in the center of your relationship?	How will you teach your kids the things of God?
What church will we go to and why?	How will you serve your local church together
How will your devotional time look alone?	How will you do devotions with your family?

Questions on Sex and Temptations.

95. What are your thoughts on waiting until marriage for sex? Cloud, Cement, Corp
96. How do you handle temptations? Cloud, Cement, Corp

This is so important to know and to observe because a pure life is sure life. If you want God to favor you; you must honor his principles on remaining faithful. This is not just for sex but for every area. I'm not saying you must work for God's love or favor, but you must work from it meaning if you truly love him you will not do anything that will separate you from him. Sin separates. It separates you from God flowing through you at a high level, it separates the promises of God from you, and it separates you from being the you He desires for you to be. Sex though is the one sin God says damages you more so than any another sin (1 Cor. 6:18) due to its ability to affect all of you (mind, emotions, and body). Sex was designed to be the last wedding gift you receive on your wedding day. It was designed for a husband and a wife to enjoy as long as they desire to bring them closer together. Sex is only safe in a marriage where both the husband and the wife are completely submitted to God no other place is sex safe. Anytime sex is experienced outside of this equation immediate destruction happens.

You may not notice it right away through a STD Sexually transmitted disease, but you will immediately feel its effect as a Soul Transmitted Disease. Every sexual encounter transfers something into your soul. Right now, you can remember every sexual experience you've had, and if you can't, you can surely remember the void that led you to open yourself up to have so many partners. Every significant sexual encounter is wrapped with an emotion which dictates the rhythm you are on now. Many people are on a lust rhythm, not a purity rhythm. They are led by lust more than they are their desire to be pure. Lust has no boundaries and it will continue to drag you down its path. If a person is not willing to wait for sex, then their lack of waiting reveals their lack of self-control.

Waiting is proof of self-control. If a person can patiently, keyword patiently, wait for sex then that person is a person that can really support you. Impatience is the fruit of impulsiveness. When a person awakens love before its time and keeps it awake for long periods of time that person's body will always be triggered sexually, and if that person is always sexually triggered then they will always be led by that trigger. Sex is a drug, and some people can't function until they have had it. This way of life is not a fun life to live or be in a relationship with. Observe the person you are with and see where their eyes, hands, and words go. People will say whatever they think you would like to hear to get you comfortable with them and once you are comfortable with them they will try and test your commitments. Never get comfortable with a person that doesn't share your commitments because they will try and corrode your commitments in time of comfort to get you to consent in a sexual practice you once said you wouldn't do. Lust lies and lust desires to lie with you to consume you. Your body is a gift, and it was only meant to be unwrapped by your husband or wife. One of the gateways to our souls are our sexual organs don't let anyone enter that way without saying I Do!

Never forget; actions speak louder than words!

How do you handle temptations?

A very important question! A question where you must witness the answered lived out. We will always be confronted with these two things

1. Test and
2. Temptations.

The state of your heart will reveal what is presented to you. Both things were designed to pull something out of you and whatever response you give it will determine its agenda. God sends test the devil sends temptations. God wants to pull faith out of you the devil wants to pull filth out of you. The quality of your heart will always determine how you answer the questions presented to you. Now not everything that crosses your path has a sender because in life you will bump into or face multiple things that weren't specifically sent to you, but the state of your heart will always reveal if it's a temptation or a test. For instance; if there is lust in your heart the lust in your heart will be tempted by the woman or man that is flirting with you. But if there is purity in your heart, your purity will see them as a test and you passing that test will cause you to level up in your purity. You are either levelling up or levelling down, and it all boils down to state of your heart. What's in there because whatever is in there will either set you up to succeed or to fail.

What are their views on sex before marriage?	
Their words say	Their actions say

| What are your views on sex before marriage |||

What is testing them?	What is tempting them?

How do they respond when tested and tempted?	Poorly	Fairly	Properly

What do these results say about what's in their heart?

What is testing you?	What is tempting you?

How do you respond when tested and tempted?	Poorly	Fairly	Properly

What do these results say about what's in your heart?

What do you need to do to pass these test and to avoid these temptations?

Questions on Spiritual Warfare

97. Are you aware of spiritual warfare if so how do you handle warfare in your life? Cloud, Cement

How a person handles warfare is important. Whether you like it or not you cannot escape the spiritual world. In some way or fashion, you will cross the paths or the plots of a demon. There are demons assigned to you to distract, derail and destroy you. Their goal is to distract you from what's most important, derail you from pursuing your purpose and destroy the purity and innocence of everything connected to you. So many believers are completely unaware of how to handle demons. They don't know who they are in Christ and they don't know how to use their weapons. They are completely unaware of that world. If you plan to do anything for God even if it's small; expect resistance. If you plan to be pure or present any image of God expect resistance. They do not want the ways of God to be seen because when people see the fruit of doing things God's way they will inquire on how to do it Gods way.

Right now, you are in the middle of a war and you must decide how you plan to fight in it. There is nothing worse as far as a relationship than being in one with someone who is completely naive of what's really going on. You need to be with someone or pray that the one you are married to comes into the knowledge of how to war in the spirit realm because it is vitally important. I go into greater detail in my book World War M3 on this topic feel free to pick it up on Amazon today so you can better understand spiritual warfare or simply head over to YouTube and type in Joshua Eze Spiritual warfare and you will see a list of my videos on the topic pop up. Feel free to watch it with your husband, wife or prospect and discuss the questions below.

How much do you know about spiritual warfare? →	Nothing at all	A little bit	A lot
How much do they know about spiritual warfare? →	Nothing at all	A little bit	A lot
At what level are you doing things for the kingdom of God? →	Low level	Moderate level	High level
At what level are they doing things for the kingdom of God? →	Low Level	Moderate Level	High level

What kind of resistances or attacks are you facing?

What must you do to cover and protect your family, marriage and property from warfare?

Questions on the Lord Leading

98. What do you feel the Lord leading you to do with your life? Cloud
99. What are some things you wrestle with God with? Cloud, Cement, Corp

Knowing what a person feels God wants them to do is important because it will let you know what their purpose and passions are. This is vital information to know because you will be able to see if you guys passions and purposes' align. A car with bad alignment is not a car you want to ride in or drive; the same is for a relationship you don't want to head off in one direction and then find out you guys were not aligned properly. Your poor alignment will have you switching in and out of lanes you were never meant to drive in. Those that love God let God

152

lead even if he leads them away from something they love. It's crazy how many of us are trying to resuscitate something God killed. God either resurrects or removes himself from dead things and if God wants something to die it will die and if you choose to stay around a dead thing then you to will be a dead, lifeless and purposeless thing. Let God lead you and let God lead them and if you all are led away from each other let it happen because time will let you know why it was led away.

Wrestling

There is not one person on this earth that hasn't or will eventually wrestle with God. Every sinner and every saint is either currently wrestling or will eventually wrestle with God and God is ok with that. Life was designed to be one of discovery. God is not hidden or desires to hide he wants to be sought after, but the only thing keeping many of us from seeing the obvious are the obstacles we allow to impede our vision. For those that are married, it is important to allow grace to reign in your marriage because the grace that helped you wrestle through the tough things of your life will be same Grace God uses through you to help your spouse wrestle with what they are wrestling with. Life is full of surprises some good and some bad. The bad though are the toughest ones to wrestle through. It's hard to wrestle with the idea of pain, sudden deaths, the loss of a child, poverty, etc. but what we must understand is that God is in control, and everything is connected to a plan that our human minds will never fully understand. I don't have all the answers and no one under the Son does but what we do have when connected to God is his love, grace, mercy and peace which are all communicating harmoniously that we are undeserved but welcomed individuals who have access to a father, through repentance, that cares and has already calculated a plan to help you grow out of this dark place. If you are that one wrestling with God tag a person in the ring to help you process what you are going through and if you are in a marriage or a relationship with a person that is struggling make sure you jump in their ring with love, peace, grace, and mercy!

What do they feel God is leading them to do?	What do you feel God is leading you to do?		
Do they match in any way? →	Yes	Kind of	Nope
What are they wrestling with?	How can you help them?		

What you are wrestling with?	How would you like to receive help?

PAST, PRESENT AND POTENTIAL

How old are you? Cloud

Their Age	Your Age	Years in between

When is your birthday? Cloud

Their Birthday:	Your Birthday:

What college or high school did you go to? Cloud

Their High School:	Their College:
Your High School:	Your College:

What do you most admire and why? Cloud, Cement

Their Answer:	Your Answer:

Where do you work or what type of business do you own? Cloud

Their Answer:

What city did you grow up in? Cloud

Their City →	

Do you have your own Car? Cloud

Do they own their own car?	Yes	No

Do you like to go out on dates? Cloud

Do they like to go on dates?	Yes	No

What were you like as a kid? Cloud, Cement

What were they like as a kid?

What were you like as a kid?

111. How do you view life right now? Cloud, Cement, Corp

How do they view life right now?	How do you view life right now?

Past Relationships

112.   Have they ever been married, divorced or separated? Cloud, Cement, Corp

Knowing this is important because it will let you know the reason why their relationship failed and if they will repeat their cause to why it failed and will let you know if they are married now which will lend to an immediate red and white flag.

| What have they experienced? → | Married | Divorced | Separated | Neither |

Questions on Children

113.   Do they have children? If so how many? Cloud, Cement, Corp
114.   Do you want children why or why not? Cloud Cement, Corp
116.   Do you want children if so how many?

Very important question! The answer will help you dig deep to see if you have the grace to attach yourself to their already existing family and to see if their desires for children matches your desires or the lack there of.

Do they have children if so how many →			#
Names of Children			
1			
2			
3			
4			
5			
Do you have children if so how many →			#
Names of Children			
1			
2			
3			
4			
5			
Do they want children? →	Yes	No	If so how many: #
Do you want children? →	Yes	No	If so how many: #

159

Them: why or why not	You: why or why not

Questions on Credit.

117. What is their credit score? Cement, Corp
118. What is your credit score?
119. What are you guys plan to raise it or maintain it?

Only ask this question when the relationship is heading towards engagement and marriage or in other words the confirmed by God cement/ corporation stage. Not everyone's current low credit score reflects their level of maturity now. The goal is to be with someone who is aggressively aiming to grow their credit and eliminate the poor habits that may have caused it to fall. So many people rule out people due to this even though this is very important, but people evolve and grow, and as long as they are pushing to raise that score up then they are cool.

What is their credit score →	
What is your credit score →	

Questions on Anger Management

120. How do you handle anger? Cloud, Cement
121. Have you ever hit a woman/ man? Cloud, Cement
122. Do you have a history of verbal abuse? Cloud, Cement
123. What are your current struggles? Cloud Cement, Corp
124. How do you handle sadness? Cloud, cement
125. How do you handle fear? Cloud, Cement
126. What areas of sin are you currently struggling with? Cement, Corp
127. What negative thing in your past is affecting your life right now? Cloud, Cement, Corp

Self-hate is real and a lot of people through not loving themselves lash out and hurt others. God cares about how we process our emotions. People who abuse others are tormented individuals. They hate themselves, and their hate either impulsively hurt others or intentionally hurt others meaning some people who hate themselves really don't want to hurt anyone, but the hate for themselves inside of them rages out in moments of rage and hurts those connected to them. Others express their hate intentionally trying to bring others down to their level and utilize their real hate and fake love to manipulate others to stay around. Either way, it is not safe to be around someone who is abusive whether physically or verbally.

They are self-haters and will use their hate for themselves to hurt you. Only God can heal those who do not love themselves. Your love can not help them. Don't let your "love" lure you into a place of danger. Don't just ask these questions observe their answers. Observe how they respond to minor aggravations like while driving or with someone that makes a minor mistake. If they are screaming and yelling irrationally over something small, then what will they do when something big happens? Knowing what a person is currently struggling with and observing how they handle minor and major aggravations will help you determine when to make an early exit. Self-control is a fruit of the spirit, and it's an important one, but like I always say the fruit of the spirit is one fruit comprised of multiple seeds meaning you can't express one without the other. You can't be self-controlled if you are not loving, kind, patient, or tender. It's impossible; they all work together.

Bottled up rage will always hit the one its closes to. Really observe how they process their emotions because any emotion that is not processed will turn into abusive behavior. No one deserves to be hit physically or verbally anyone who does so is a coward and doesn't deserve to be in a relationship now. They need God, and there is nothing you can do but love and pray for them from a distance. You can't save them only Jesus can. If you are in a verbal and physically abusive relationship leave now! If that means you work an extra job do it if that means you have to move back home with mama do it. You are too valuable to be in a relationship with someone that doesn't love themselves. Pray, prepare, pack, and pull off. Those that choose to stay in these situations too struggle with self-hate. You must love yourself enough to remove yourself from things that are truly beneath you. Is he or she really all of that? And if you are the abuser seek help because what you are doing is cowardly and unacceptable. Run to God and let him renew you.

Take the time to really assess if the person you are with is a self-hater and if you are a self-hater.

Have they shown signs of verbal or physical abuse?		Yes	Kind of	Not yet
If so how severe?	Not at all	Mild	Severe	
If so why are you choosing to stay?				
Have you shown signs of verbal or physical abuse?		Yes	Kind of	Not yet
If so how severe?	Not at all	Mild	Severe	
If so are you looking for help?				

Question on STD

128.   Do you have any STD's that I need to know about? Cloud, Cement, Corp

Know this quick because you don't' want the mismanagement of their temple to damage yours. Everyone has made mistakes, and everyone deserves a second chance at love just make sure you are well informed and led by God.

Do they have an STD →	No	Not sure yet	Yes
Do you have an STD →	No	Not sure yet	Yes
If so have you told your significant other?		Yes	No

162

Questions on Intentions

129.   What are their intentions with you? Cloud, Cement, Corp
130.   What are your intentions with them?

Intentions are everything. Your time is too valuable to be wasted. You need to know upfront what their intentions are with you at each stage of the relationship so that you can determine what you must do. People get comfortable, and sometimes you need to shake them out of their complacency and ask so that you guys can be on the same sentence and on the same word. Communication is key to all relationships. Being on the same page is cool but being on the same word in the same sentence is even better.

What are their intentions with you?	What are your intentions with them?

Question on how many bf/gf

131.   How many relationships have they been in? Cloud, Cement, Corp

Great question to know the answer to. Too many and too little can both raise some eyebrows. Too many can raise the concern about whether this person is still trying to find him or herself or if he or she is just insane. Too little can raise the concern of experience and whether they understand what it takes to operate and function in a relationship. Take some time to hear their reasons and let their actions reveal to you if you should be the one of many or the first one.

How many boyfriends or girlfriends have they had?	#
How many boyfriends or girlfriends have you had?	#

How is their amount of relationships affecting your relationship now?	How is your amount of relationships affecting your relationship now?

$$$

132.   How well do you handle money? Cloud, Cement Corp

If you truly want to know about a person check their bank statements and their money trail. Their money trail will always lead to their idols or what they love the most. Money matters and how a person spends money will determine how far a family will go. So many people are hindered from their destiny due to debt, and the debt they are in are for stupid reasons. A God dream will never lead you into debt; it can lead you out of it but it surely won't lead you into it. So many people are spending for the moment and not for the future. Your spending habits now will determine what you will be able to afford or experience later. Take the time to listen and observe how they spend their money because where you find their money, you will find your heart. Also, make sure you take the time to look at your money trail and audit how you spend money because your money is where your heart is.

PS: there is nothing wrong with liking and having nice things just make sure it is not an obsession and make sure you are not spending dream money. So many people look like they are living a dream but are really living a nightmare. They are spending to impress instead of pressing towards their goals. I rather work my money instead of wear my money. Money is not evil the love of it is, and your carnal love will leave you broke if you are not careful.

How well do they manage money? →	Not too well	Their ok with money	They're really good with money
How well do you manage money? →	Not too well	I'm ok with money	I'm really good with money

What does your bank statements say about you?	What do you spend the most money on?
What does their bank statements say about them?	What do they spend the most money on?

Question on wife making more.

133.   Can you handle if your wife makes more than you? Cloud, Cement

Not too many men can handle this, and it's a shame. You can still lead your home if your wife makes more than you. If she loves God and honors the role God desires for her to commit to, then she will not have a problem in letting you be the leader. But you must be whole yourself. Both parties must accept the role God has given to each gender and let him navigate the nuances of the relationship. A woman making more than a man shouldn't make a man feel lesser than; it should make him proud. That's why fellas, it's important for you to be with a woman who is gentle, discerning and who is committed to God so you won't have to deal with a power struggle. So many women are using their looks and their status to force themselves as the leader of their homes causing the man to feel useless.

Fellas read this closely → run away from any woman who is more consumed with her looks, her status or her pride than she is the things of God because she will not submit to you. She will be little you and cause you to feel like nothing. Keep hustling and grinding and let God bring you a woman who will encourage you and allow you to be the man He desires for you to be. And, ladies read this closely → run away from any man who is too insecure to celebrate your wins and accomplishments and who is too dumb to see that your money is there to help the family. If he is struggling with the idea of you making more than him then he is not equipped to lead because a leader knows how to recognize resources. Keep being resourceful and making your money homie because God will send you a man that you won't mind submitting yourself and your resources to him 😊.

Questions on passions and goals!

134. What's your passion? Cloud, Cement, Corp
135. What kind of an impact do you want to make? Cloud, Cement
136. What are your current goals concerning your life? Cloud, Cement
137. What are your short/long-term goals? Cloud, Cement
138. If money wasn't an issue what would you do right now? Cloud, Cement, Corp
139. Where do you see yourself in 5 years? Cloud, Cement, Corp
140. Where do you see yourself in 10 years? Cloud, Cement, Corp

I truly believe that your way out of poverty or out of any systematic oppression is buried by God inside of you. The only thing that is keeping that power from coming out of some of us is or faith in God. Life is a powerful force and it's important that we learn how to manage it and learn how our significant other manages it as well. We all have passions, and our passions are the fuel that keeps our faith flowing. The problems lie though in what our faith is in? Whoever has your faith is the one that is responsible for keeping you faithful. When your hope and joy is in God, and you desire to advance his kingdom in whatever industry you are passionate about then when you feel low he will refuel you. But if your faith is in what this person can do or what this ideal life will do for you, then you will find out that at the end of that road is **emptiness**. His will; will fill. Fulfillment is the name of the game ladies and gentlemen, and you must ask yourself and the one you plan to be with or are married to now; what are you here to do?

The questions above are important questions for you to ask and for you to answer. They will help you see deep into the reservoir of you and your significant others heart to see what fuels them. Knowing their passion knowing where they want to make an impact and knowing what their goals are, are essential in knowing if you guys are **compatible**. You were never designed to complete anyone you were designed to complement them. So many people are looking for people to complete them instead of leaning on the only one that can complete them, and his name is Jesus. He completes we compliment.

Take some time to listen to each other's dreams and see what you both have in common and be sure to listen to see if they want you to complete their dreams or compliment their dreams.

What is their passion in life?	What is your passion in life?
What kind of an impact do they want to make?	What kind of an impact do you want to make?
If money wasn't an issue what would they do right now?	If money wasn't an issue what would you do right now?
What are their current goals concerning their life?	What are your current goals concerning your life?

Where do they see yourself in 5 and 10 years?	Where do you see yourself in 5 and 10 years?

Question on Time management.

141.   On the regular how do you use your time? Cloud, Cement, Corp

Time is life and time is money and how someone uses their time will determine what kind of life they will live and how much money they will make. Time is the only thing you can never get back. None of us can relive a wasted day, and with that being true we should endeavor, never to waste a day. Every marriage should have as one of their core traits; discipline. Discipline ensures dreams comes to past. Without discipline everything unravels. Observe their work ethic and their discipline and how they spend their time because how they spend their time will affect what kind of married life you will have and how much your marriage will be worth. $

Calculate for the next week how you spend your time and at the end calculate how much of your time was used productively vs wasted.

Exact time: List below everything you do in a given day and estimate how much time you spend on each thing. Ex: eating, sleeping, on the phone, social media etc.			
Day One		Day Two	
Activity	Time	Activity	Time
How much time was productive?		How much time was productive?	
How much time was wasted?		How much time was wasted?	

Day Three		Day Four	
Activity	Time	Activity	Time
How much time was productive?		How much time was productive?	
How much time was wasted?		How much time was wasted?	

Day Five		Day Six	
Activity	Time	Activity	Time

How much time was productive?		How much time was productive?	
How much time was wasted?		How much time was wasted?	
Day Seven		Day Eight	
Activity	Time	Activity	Time
How much time was productive?		How much time was productive?	
How much time was wasted?		How much time was wasted?	

Questions on Accountability.

142.   Who is your accountability partner? Cloud, cement, Corp
143.   What are your strengths and weaknesses? Cloud, Cement, Corp

A person without accountability is not fit to be a husband or a wife. Both parties must have a seasoned person of the same sex or a seasoned couple that holds them accountable and checks on them. Accountability is giving a person or persons the ability to account for your life in all areas both strong and weak. You need a person or a community of people that can hold you accountable in every significant area of your life. Your strengths need accountability and your weaknesses. Sin and demons have no respecter of area and they will hunt down your strengths just as quickly as they do your weaknesses. Each area needs an accountability partner to ensure you succeed.

If you plan to advance plan to be held accountable. If this person doesn't have a credible person as their accountability partner or doesn't have an accountability partner at all then that should cause you to raise a red or yellow flag because wherever they lack accountability is the area that will be used against your relationship.

Remember the keyword for accountability is **ability**. They must be seasoned people; people who are held accountable themselves.

List below your seasoned accountability partners and how they hold you accountable.		
Accountability	Areas held accountable	Seasoned/ not seasoned

Who are their accountability and where do they hold them accountable?		
Accountability	Areas held accountable	Seasoned/ not seasoned

List below your strengths and weaknesses and beside each one write who is holding that area accountable.

Strengths		Weaknesses	
Strength	Accountability	Weakness	Accountability

List below their strengths and weaknesses and beside each one write who is holding that area accountable.

Strengths		Weaknesses	
Strength	Accountability	Weakness	Accountability

What areas above are without accountability and what must you do to guard these areas until they are held accounted for?

Prayer List

144. How can I pray for you? Cloud, cement, Corp

List their prayer request below and check off the days you prayed for them in each area.							
Prayer Request:							
D1	D2	D3	D4	D5	D6	D7	
D8	D9	D10	D11	D12	D13	D14	
D15	D16	D17	D18	D19	D20	D21	
Answered Prayer: Document how it was answered.							
Date Prayer was answered →							
Prayer Request:							
D1	D2	D3	D4	D5	D6	D7	
D8	D9	D10	D11	D12	D13	D14	
D15	D16	D17	D18	D19	D20	D21	
Answered Prayer: Document how it was answered.							
Date Prayer was answered →							
Prayer Request:							
D1	D2	D3	D4	D5	D6	D7	
D8	D9	D10	D11	D12	D13	D14	
D15	D16	D17	D18	D19	D20	D21	
Answered Prayer: Document how it was answered.							
Date Prayer was answered →							

145. What characteristics do you look for in a spouse? Cement, Corp

What are they looking for in a spouse?		
What they want. Characteristics	Do they match what they want Yes or No	Do you match what they want Yes or No

Where do you see us 5 to 10 years from now?

146. Where do you see us in 5 years? Cement, Corp
147. Where do you see us in 10 years? Cement, Corp

A relationship without a vision will perish. It's good to hear where you both see your marriage or relationship 5-10 years from now. Take some time with your wife, husband or your God-Certified boyfriend or girlfriend and develop a five year and ten-year Relationship Vision Board. Go to your local Wal-Mart or hobby lobby and pick up some arts and crafts and really create a board that you guys can see every day to inspire you all to achieve those goals utilize the box below to write buzz words that will help you plan on what to buy or how to design your board!

In 5 years we will be:

In 10 years we will be:

YOUR FAVS. THEIR FAVS.

What is your favorite color? →	
What is their favorite color? →	
What is your second favorite color? →	
What is their second favorite color? →	
What is your favorite song and why? Song: _____ Why → →→	
What is their favorite song and why? Song: _____ Why → →→	
What is your favorite movie and why? Movie: _____ Why → →→	
What is their favorite movie and why? Movie: _____ Why → →→	
What is your favorite genre of music Genre: _____ Why → →→	
What is their favorite genre of music Genre: _____ Why → →→	
What is your favorite thing to do on the weekend? _____ Why → →→	
What is their favorite thing to do on the weekend? _____ Why → →→	
What is your favorite dessert and why? Dessert: _____ Why → →→	

What is their favorite dessert and why? Dessert: _____ Why → →→	
What is your favorite bag of chips and why? _____ Why → →→	
What is their favorite bag of chips and why? _____ Why → → →	
Where do you work? Do you like it or not? _____ Why → →→	
Where do they work? Do they like it or not? _____ Why → →→	
What is your favorite attribute about yourself and why → →→	
What is their favorite attribute about themselves and why → →→	
What is your least favorite attribute about yourself and why? → →→	
What is their least favorite attribute about yourself and why? → →→	
Who are your favorite speakers? → →→	
Who are their favorite speakers? → →→	
Who is your best friend and what makes them your best friend? → →→	
Who is their best friend and what makes them their best friend? → →→	

What is your favorite car/ vehicle and why? _____ Why → →→	
What is their favorite car/ vehicle and why? _____ Why → →→	
What is your favorite city to visit and why? _____ Why → →→	
What is their favorite city to visit and why? _____ Why → →→	
What is your favorite season and why? → →→	
What is their favorite season and why? → →→	
Who is your favorite sports team and why? → →→	
Who is their favorite sports team and why? → →→	
How do you like to receive love and why? → →→	
How do they like to receive love and why? → →→	
What was your favorite cartoon growing up and why? → →→	
What was their favorite cartoon growing up and why? → →→	

What is your favorite book to read and why? _____ Why → →→	
What is their favorite book to read and why? _____ Why → →→	
What is your favorite bible verse and why? _____ Why → →→	
What is their favorite bible verse and why? _____ Why → →→	
What is your favorite shape? → →→	
What is their favorite shape? → →→	
What is the one thing you like best about them? → →→	
What is the one thing they like best about you? → →→	
What is the one thing you appreciate most about God? → →→	
What is the one thing they appreciate most about God? → →→	
What's one thing about them you wish they would never change? → →→	
What's one thing about you they wish you would never change? → →→	

What is **our** favorite hangout spot? _____ Why → →→	
What is **our** favorite movie? _____ Why → →→	
What is **our** favorite song? _____ Why → →→	
What is **our** favorite restaurant? _____ Why → →→	
Where is your favorite place to shop? Why→ →→	
Where is their favorite place to shop? Why→ →→	
What are your favorite kind of gifts to receive? → →→	
What are their favorite kind of gifts to receive? → →→	
What is your favorite book in the bible and why? → →→	
What is your favorite book in the bible and why? → →→	

Whew! The End

1-YEAR RELATIONSHIP TRACKER

This section is for those that are dating, courting or married to someone. This tracker was designed to help you focus on the details and the desired outcomes of your relationship helping you guys either grow together or grow apart. Utilize this section to set goals to vent and to journal your next year with your significant other. →

Monthly Prep 1											
Highlight or circle the current month											
JAN	FEB	MAR	APR	MAY	JUN	JUL	AUG	SEPT	OCT	NOV	DEC

Relationship Goals for this month?

In what ways do you plan to serve your significant other this month?

Monthly Progress 1				
How's the relationship going so far?	Not Good	Eh	Better	Great
Why the answer above?				
Any Red Flags so far?			No	Yes
If so what happened?				
Deal Breaker?			No	Yes
How do you honestly feel in the relationship at this moment?	Not Good	Eh	Better	Great
Why these feelings?				

What have you learned new about your significant other this month?

Favorite question asked this month?	What was their answer?

Date Night	Where did you guys go?	How was it?		
Date	Location or Activity	Good, eh, or bad		
		Good	Eh	Bad
		Good	Eh	Bad
		Good	Eh	Bad
		Good	Eh	Bad

What improvements have you and your significant other made together this month?	How did you guys celebrate?
Great moments this month	Tough moments this month

Any arguments this month if so how many?	#	
Over what?	Was it worth it?	
Were your goals for this month accomplished?	No	Yes
In what ways do you need to improve for the next month?		
Does the relationship need to end?	No	Yes
Why or why not?		

Week 1 Month 1 Journaling	Today's Date:

Week 2 Month 1 Journaling	Today's Date:

Week 3 Month 1 Journaling	Today's Date:

Week 4 Month 1 Journaling	Today's Date:

Monthly Prep 2											
Highlight or circle the current month											
JAN	FEB	MAR	APR	MAY	JUN	JUL	AUG	SEPT	OCT	NOV	DEC

Relationship Goals for this month?

In what ways do you plan to serve your significant other this month?

Monthly Progress 2				
How's the relationship going so far?	Not Good	Eh	Better	Great
Why the answer above?				
Any Red Flags so far?			No	Yes
If so what happened?				
Deal Breaker?			No	Yes
How do you honestly feel in the relationship at this moment?	Not Good	Eh	Better	Great
Why these feelings?				

What have you learned new about your significant other this month?

Favorite question asked this month?	What was their answer?

Date Night	Where did you guys go?	How was it?		
Date	Location or Activity	Good, eh, or bad		
		Good	Eh	Bad
		Good	Eh	Bad
		Good	Eh	Bad
		Good	Eh	Bad

What improvements have you and your significant other made together this month?	How did you guys celebrate?	
Great moments this month	Tough moments this month	
Any arguments this month if so how many?	#	
Over what?	Was it worth it?	
Were your goals for this month accomplished?	No	Yes
In what ways do you need to improve for the next month?		
Does the relationship need to end?	No	Yes
Why or why not?		

Week 1 Month 2 Journaling	Today's Date:

Week 2 Month 2 Journaling	Today's Date:

Week 3 Month 2 Journaling	Today's Date:

Week 4 Month 2 Journaling	Today's Date:

Monthly Prep 3
Highlight or circle the current month
JAN • FEB • MAR • APR • MAY • JUN • JUL • AUG • SEPT • OCT • NOV • DEC
Relationship Goals for this month?
In what ways do you plan to serve your significant other this month?

Monthly Progress 3				
How's the relationship going so far?	Not Good	Eh	Better	Great
Why the answer above?				
Any Red Flags so far?			No	Yes
If so what happened?				
Deal Breaker?			No	Yes
How do you honestly feel in the relationship at this moment?	Not Good	Eh	Better	Great
Why these feelings?				
What have you learned new about your significant other this month?				
Favorite question asked this month?	What was their answer?			

Date Night	Where did you guys go?	How was it?		
Date	Location or Activity	Good, eh, or bad		
		Good	Eh	Bad
		Good	Eh	Bad
		Good	Eh	Bad
		Good	Eh	Bad

What improvements have you and your significant other made together this month?	How did you guys celebrate?		
Great moments this month	Tough moments this month		
Any arguments this month if so how many?		#	
Over what?		Was it worth it?	
Were your goals for this month accomplished?		No	Yes
In what ways do you need to improve for the next month?			
Does the relationship need to end?		No	Yes
Why or why not?			

Week 1 Month 3 Journaling	Today's Date:

Week 2 Month 3 Journaling	Today's Date:

Week 3 Month 3 Journaling	Today's Date:

Week 4 Month 3 Journaling	Today's Date:

Monthly Prep 4											
Highlight or circle the current month											
JAN	FEB	MAR	APR	MAY	JUN	JUL	AUG	SEPT	OCT	NOV	DEC

Relationship Goals for this month?

In what ways do you plan to serve your significant other this month?

Monthly Progress 4

How's the relationship going so far?	Not Good	Eh	Better	Great

Why the answer above?

Any Red Flags so far?	No	Yes

If so what happened?

Deal Breaker?		No	Yes
How do you honestly feel in the relationship at this moment?	Not Good	Eh	Better	Great

Why these feelings?

What have you learned new about your significant other this month?

Favorite question asked this month?	What was their answer?

Date Night	Where did you guys go?	How was it?		
Date	Location or Activity	Good, eh, or bad		
		Good	Eh	Bad
		Good	Eh	Bad
		Good	Eh	Bad
		Good	Eh	Bad

What improvements have you and your significant other made together this month?	How did you guys celebrate?	
Great moments this month	Tough moments this month	
Any arguments this month if so how many?	#	
Over what?	Was it worth it?	
Were your goals for this month accomplished?	No	Yes
In what ways do you need to improve for the next month?		
Does the relationship need to end?	No	Yes
Why or why not?		

Week 1 Month 4 Journaling	Today's Date:

Week 2 Month 4 Journaling	Today's Date:

Week 3 Month 4 Journaling	Today's Date:

Week 4 Month 4 Journaling	Today's Date:

Monthly Prep 5
Highlight or circle the current month
JAN | FEB | MAR | APR | MAY | JUN | JUL | AUG | SEPT | OCT | NOV | DEC
Relationship Goals for this month?
In what ways do you plan to serve your significant other this month?

Monthly Progress 5				
How's the relationship going so far?	Not Good	Eh	Better	Great
Why the answer above?				
Any Red Flags so far?			No	Yes
If so what happened?				
Deal Breaker?			No	Yes
How do you honestly feel in the relationship at this moment?	Not Good	Eh	Better	Great
Why these feelings?				
What have you learned new about your significant other this month?				

Favorite question asked this month?	What was their answer?

Date Night	Where did you guys go?	How was it?		
Date	Location or Activity	Good, eh, or bad		
		Good	Eh	Bad
		Good	Eh	Bad
		Good	Eh	Bad
		Good	Eh	Bad

What improvements have you and your significant other made together this month?	How did you guys celebrate?
Great moments this month	Tough moments this month

Any arguments this month if so how many?	#	
Over what?	Was it worth it?	
Were your goals for this month accomplished?	No	Yes
In what ways do you need to improve for the next month?		
Does the relationship need to end?	No	Yes
Why or why not?		

Week 1 Month 5 Journaling	Today's Date:

Week 2 Month 5 Journaling	Today's Date:

Week 3 Month 5 Journaling	Today's Date:

Week 4 Month 5 Journaling	Today's Date:

Monthly Prep 6											
Highlight or circle the current month											
JAN	FEB	MAR	APR	MAY	JUN	JUL	AUG	SEPT	OCT	NOV	DEC
Relationship Goals for this month?											
In what ways do you plan to serve your significant other this month?											

Monthly Progress 6				
How's the relationship going so far?	Not Good	Eh	Better	Great
Why the answer above?				
Any Red Flags so far?			No	Yes
If so what happened?				
Deal Breaker?			No	Yes
How do you honestly feel in the relationship at this moment?	Not Good	Eh	Better	Great
Why these feelings?				
What have you learned new about your significant other this month?				
Favorite question asked this month?	What was their answer?			

Date Night	Where did you guys go?	How was it?		
Date	Location or Activity	Good, eh, or bad		
		Good	Eh	Bad
		Good	Eh	Bad
		Good	Eh	Bad
		Good	Eh	Bad

What improvements have you and your significant other made together this month?	How did you guys celebrate?		
Great moments this month	Tough moments this month		
Any arguments this month if so how many?	#		
Over what?	Was it worth it?		
Were your goals for this month accomplished?	No	Yes	
In what ways do you need to improve for the next month?			
Does the relationship need to end?	No	Yes	
Why or why not?			

Week 1 Month 6 Journaling	Today's Date:

Week 2 Month 6 Journaling	Today's Date:

Week 3 Month 6 Journaling	Today's Date:

Week 4 Month 6 Journaling	Today's Date:

Monthly Prep 7
Highlight or circle the current month
JAN | FEB | MAR | APR | MAY | JUN | JUL | AUG | SEPT | OCT | NOV | DEC
Relationship Goals for this month?
In what ways do you plan to serve your significant other this month?

Monthly Progress 7				
How's the relationship going so far?	Not Good	Eh	Better	Great
Why the answer above?				
Any Red Flags so far?			No	Yes
If so what happened?				
Deal Breaker?			No	Yes
How do you honestly feel in the relationship at this moment?	Not Good	Eh	Better	Great
Why these feelings?				
What have you learned new about your significant other this month?				

Favorite question asked this month?	What was their answer?

Date Night	Where did you guys go?	How was it?		
Date	Location or Activity	Good, eh, or bad		
		Good	Eh	Bad
		Good	Eh	Bad
		Good	Eh	Bad
		Good	Eh	Bad

What improvements have you and your significant other made together this month?	How did you guys celebrate?	
Great moments this month	Tough moments this month	
Any arguments this month if so how many?	#	
Over what?	Was it worth it?	
Were your goals for this month accomplished?	No	Yes
In what ways do you need to improve for the next month?		
Does the relationship need to end?	No	Yes
Why or why not?		

Week 1 Month 7 Journaling	Today's Date:

Week 2 Month 7 Journaling	Today's Date:

Week 3 Month 7 Journaling	Today's Date:

Week 4 Month 7 Journaling	Today's Date:

Monthly Prep 8

Highlight or circle the current month

| JAN | FEB | MAR | APR | MAY | JUN | JUL | AUG | SEPT | OCT | NOV | DEC |

Relationship Goals for this month?

In what ways do you plan to serve your significant other this month?

Monthly Progress 8

| How's the relationship going so far? | Not Good | Eh | Better | Great |

Why the answer above?

| Any Red Flags so far? | No | Yes |

If so what happened?

| Deal Breaker? | No | Yes |
| How do you honestly feel in the relationship at this moment? | Not Good | Eh | Better | Great |

Why these feelings?

What have you learned new about your significant other this month?

| Favorite question asked this month? | What was their answer? |

Date Night	Where did you guys go?	How was it?		
Date	Location or Activity	Good, eh, or bad		
		Good	Eh	Bad
		Good	Eh	Bad
		Good	Eh	Bad
		Good	Eh	Bad

What improvements have you and your significant other made together this month?	How did you guys celebrate?

Great moments this month	Tough moments this month

Any arguments this month if so how many?	#	
Over what?	Was it worth it?	

Were your goals for this month accomplished?	No	Yes
In what ways do you need to improve for the next month?		

Does the relationship need to end?	No	Yes
Why or why not?		

Week 1 Month 8 Journaling	Today's Date:

Week 2 Month 8 Journaling	Today's Date:

Week 3 Month 8 Journaling	Today's Date:

Week 4 Month 8 Journaling	Today's Date:

Monthly Prep 9											
Highlight or circle the current month											
JAN	FEB	MAR	APR	MAY	JUN	JUL	AUG	SEPT	OCT	NOV	DEC

Relationship Goals for this month?

In what ways do you plan to serve your significant other this month?

Monthly Progress 9				
How's the relationship going so far?	Not Good	Eh	Better	Great
Why the answer above?				
Any Red Flags so far?			No	Yes
If so what happened?				
Deal Breaker?			No	Yes
How do you honestly feel in the relationship at this moment?	Not Good	Eh	Better	Great
Why these feelings?				
What have you learned new about your significant other this month?				

Favorite question asked this month?	What was their answer?

Date Night	Where did you guys go?	How was it?		
Date	Location or Activity	Good, eh, or bad		
		Good	Eh	Bad
		Good	Eh	Bad
		Good	Eh	Bad
		Good	Eh	Bad

What improvements have you and your significant other made together this month?	How did you guys celebrate?	
Great moments this month	Tough moments this month	
Any arguments this month if so how many?	#	
Over what?	Was it worth it?	
Were your goals for this month accomplished?	No	Yes
In what ways do you need to improve for the next month?		
Does the relationship need to end?	No	Yes
Why or why not?		

Week 1 Month 9 Journaling	Today's Date:

Week 2 Month 9 Journaling	Today's Date:

Week 3 Month 9 Journaling	Today's Date:

Week 4 Month 9 Journaling	Today's Date:

Monthly Prep 10											
Highlight or circle the current month											
JAN	FEB	MAR	APR	MAY	JUN	JUL	AUG	SEPT	OCT	NOV	DEC

Relationship Goals for this month?

In what ways do you plan to serve your significant other this month?

Monthly Progress 10				
How's the relationship going so far?	Not Good	Eh	Better	Great
Why the answer above?				
Any Red Flags so far?			No	Yes
If so what happened?				
Deal Breaker?			No	Yes
How do you honestly feel in the relationship at this moment?	Not Good	Eh	Better	Great
Why these feelings?				

What have you learned new about your significant other this month?

Favorite question asked this month?	What was their answer?

Date Night	Where did you guys go?	How was it?		
Date	Location or Activity	Good, eh, or bad		
		Good	Eh	Bad
		Good	Eh	Bad
		Good	Eh	Bad
		Good	Eh	Bad

What improvements have you and your significant other made together this month?	How did you guys celebrate?	
Great moments this month	Tough moments this month	
Any arguments this month if so how many?	#	
Over what?	Was it worth it?	
Were your goals for this month accomplished?	No	Yes
In what ways do you need to improve for the next month?		
Does the relationship need to end?	No	Yes
Why or why not?		

Week 1 Month 10 Journaling	Today's Date:

Week 2 Month 10 Journaling	Today's Date:

Week 3 Month 10 Journaling	Today's Date:

Week 4 Month 10 Journaling	Today's Date:

Monthly Prep 11											
Highlight or circle the current month											
JAN	FEB	MAR	APR	MAY	JUN	JUL	AUG	SEPT	OCT	NOV	DEC
Relationship Goals for this month?											
In what ways do you plan to serve your significant other this month?											

Monthly Progress 11				
How's the relationship going so far?	Not Good	Eh	Better	Great
Why the answer above?				
Any Red Flags so far?			No	Yes
If so what happened?				
Deal Breaker?			No	Yes
How do you honestly feel in the relationship at this moment?	Not Good	Eh	Better	Great
Why these feelings?				
What have you learned new about your significant other this month?				

Favorite question asked this month?	What was their answer?

Date Night	Where did you guys go?	How was it?		
Date	Location or Activity	Good, eh, or bad		
		Good	Eh	Bad
		Good	Eh	Bad
		Good	Eh	Bad
		Good	Eh	Bad

What improvements have you and your significant other made together this month?	How did you guys celebrate?
Great moments this month	Tough moments this month

Any arguments this month if so how many?	#
Over what?	Was it worth it?

Were your goals for this month accomplished?	No	Yes
In what ways do you need to improve for the next month?		

Does the relationship need to end?	No	Yes
Why or why not?		

Week 1 Month 11 Journaling	Today's Date:

Week 2 Month 11 Journaling	Today's Date:

Week 3 Month 11 Journaling	Today's Date:

Week 4 Month 11 Journaling	Today's Date:

Monthly Prep 12

Highlight or circle the current month

JAN	FEB	MAR	APR	MAY	JUN	JUL	AUG	SEPT	OCT	NOV	DEC

Relationship Goals for this month?

In what ways do you plan to serve your significant other this month?

Monthly Progress 12

How's the relationship going so far?	Not Good	Eh	Better	Great

Why the answer above?

Any Red Flags so far?	No	Yes

If so what happened?

Deal Breaker?		No	Yes
How do you honestly feel in the relationship at this moment?	Not Good	Eh	Better	Great

Why these feelings?

What have you learned new about your significant other this month?

Favorite question asked this month?	What was their answer?

Date Night	Where did you guys go?	How was it?		
Date	Location or Activity	Good, eh, or bad		
		Good	Eh	Bad
		Good	Eh	Bad
		Good	Eh	Bad
		Good	Eh	Bad

What improvements have you and your significant other made together this month?	How did you guys celebrate?		
Great moments this month	Tough moments this month		
Any arguments this month if so how many?	#		
Over what?	Was it worth it?		
Were your goals for this month accomplished?		No	Yes
In what ways do you need to improve for the next month?			
Does the relationship need to end?		No	Yes
Why or why not?			

Week 1 Month 12 Journaling	Today's Date:

Week 2 Month 12 Journaling	Today's Date:

Week 3 Month 12 Journaling	Today's Date:

Week 4 Month 12 Journaling	Today's Date:

1-YEAR OFF-SEASON TRACKER

This section is for those that are single and are preparing to mingle. This tracker was designed to help you focus on the details and the desired outcomes of your life helping you to grow in the things of God, your purpose and into the person you will need to be to compliment someone. Utilize this section to set goals to vent and to journal your next year single or possibly starting a new relationship.
↓

Before you start: Answer the Following

Where are you on a scale of 1-10 in your relationship with God right now?									
1	2	3	4	5	6	7	8	9	10
Where are you on a scale of 1-10 in preparation for a significant other?									
1	2	3	4	5	6	7	8	9	10
Where are you on a scale of 1-10 in finishing the assignment of your single years?									
1	2	3	4	5	6	7	8	9	10

What areas are you looking to improve on this year?
1
2
3
4
5
Current struggles or vices
1
2
3
4
5
What is your craft? What are you here to do on earth?

Monthly Prep 1											
Highlight or circle the current month											
JAN	FEB	MAR	APR	MAY	JUN	JUL	AUG	SEPT	OCT	NOV	DEC
Personal Goals and desired outcomes for this month											

Verse Marinade for the month (Memorize) →	2 Timothy 2:4
Bible Reading for the month →	The Book of Matthew

Monthly Progress 1

How do you view your singleness at this moment?	Not good	Ok	Great
Why these feelings?			

What good, bad or ugly things showed up in your heart this month?

Good	Bad	Ugly

What do you need to do to improve in each area?

Levelled up: Did you level up or leveled down this month:

	Levelled Up	Levelled Down	# 1-10
In Contentment			
In your Relationship w/ God			
With your Vices or Struggles			
On working on your craft			
With your family			
With the fruits of the spirit			

Any prospects this month? If So who? →			
Did you accomplish your goals this month?		Yes	No
Did you receive the desired outcomes for this month		Yes	No
If no what interfered?	If yes what helped?		

How was week One? – Journal Entry	How was week Two? – Journal Entry

Days I prayed, read my bible, worked on my craft and fellowshipped. (Circle)

PRAYED	D1	D2	D3	D4	D5	D6	D7	D8	D9	D10	D11	D12	D13	D14
READ	D1	D2	D3	D4	D5	D6	D7	D8	D9	D10	D11	D12	D13	D14
CRAFT	D1	D2	D3	D4	D5	D6	D7	D8	D9	D10	D11	D12	D13	D14
FELLOW	D1	D2	D3	D4	D5	D6	D7	D8	D9	D10	D11	D12	D13	D14

How was week Three? – Journal Entry	How was week Four? – Journal Entry

Days I prayed, read my bible, worked on my craft and fellowshipped.

PRAYED	D1	D2	D3	D4	D5	D6	D7	D8	D9	D10	D11	D12	D13	D14
READ	D1	D2	D3	D4	D5	D6	D7	D8	D9	D10	D11	D12	D13	D14
CRAFT	D1	D2	D3	D4	D5	D6	D7	D8	D9	D10	D11	D12	D13	D14
FELLOW	D1	D2	D3	D4	D5	D6	D7	D8	D9	D10	D11	D12	D13	D14

Monthly Prep 2											
Highlight or circle the current month											
JAN	FEB	MAR	APR	MAY	JUN	JUL	AUG	SEPT	OCT	NOV	DEC
Personal Goals and desired outcomes for this month											

Verse Marinade for the month (Memorize) →	Hebrews 13:5
Bible Reading for the month →	The Book of Mark

Monthly Progress 2

How do you view your singleness at this moment?		Not good	Ok	Great
Why these feelings?				

What good, bad or ugly things showed up in your heart this month?		
Good	Bad	Ugly

What do you need to do to improve in each area?

Levelled up: Did you level up or leveled down this month:			
In Contentment	Levelled Up	Levelled Down	# 1-10
In your Relationship w/ God			
With your Vices or Struggles			
On working on your craft			
With your family			
With the fruits of the spirit			

Any prospects this month? If So who? →			
Did you accomplish your goals this month?		Yes	No
Did you receive the desired outcomes for this month		Yes	No
If no what interfered?	If yes what helped?		

How was week One? – Journal Entry	How was week Two? – Journal Entry

Days I prayed, read my bible, worked on my craft and fellowshipped. (Circle)

PRAYED	D1	D2	D3	D4	D5	D6	D7	D8	D9	D10	D11	D12	D13	D14
READ	D1	D2	D3	D4	D5	D6	D7	D8	D9	D10	D11	D12	D13	D14
CRAFT	D1	D2	D3	D4	D5	D6	D7	D8	D9	D10	D11	D12	D13	D14
FELLOW	D1	D2	D3	D4	D5	D6	D7	D8	D9	D10	D11	D12	D13	D14

How was week Three? – Journal Entry	How was week Four? – Journal Entry

Days I prayed, read my bible, worked on my craft and fellowshipped.

PRAYED	D1	D2	D3	D4	D5	D6	D7	D8	D9	D10	D11	D12	D13	D14
READ	D1	D2	D3	D4	D5	D6	D7	D8	D9	D10	D11	D12	D13	D14
CRAFT	D1	D2	D3	D4	D5	D6	D7	D8	D9	D10	D11	D12	D13	D14
FELLOW	D1	D2	D3	D4	D5	D6	D7	D8	D9	D10	D11	D12	D13	D14

Monthly Prep 3

Highlight or circle the current month

JAN	FEB	MAR	APR	MAY	JUN	JUL	AUG	SEPT	OCT	NOV	DEC

Personal Goals and desired outcomes for this month

Verse Marinade for the month (Memorize) →	Proverbs 24:27
Bible Reading for the month →	The Book of Luke

Monthly Progress 3

How do you view your singleness at this moment?	Not good	Ok	Great

Why these feelings?

What good, bad or ugly things showed up in your heart this month?

Good	Bad	Ugly

What do you need to do to improve in each area?

Levelled up: Did you level up or leveled down this month:

	Levelled Up	Levelled Down	# 1-10
In Contentment			
In your Relationship w/ God			
With your Vices or Struggles			
On working on your craft			
With your family			
With the fruits of the spirit			
Any prospects this month? If So who? →			
Did you accomplish your goals this month?		Yes	No
Did you receive the desired outcomes for this month		Yes	No

If no what interfered?	If yes what helped?

How was week One? – Journal Entry	How was week Two? – Journal Entry

Days I prayed, read my bible, worked on my craft and fellowshipped. (Circle)

PRAYED	D1	D2	D3	D4	D5	D6	D7	D8	D9	D10	D11	D12	D13	D14
READ	D1	D2	D3	D4	D5	D6	D7	D8	D9	D10	D11	D12	D13	D14
CRAFT	D1	D2	D3	D4	D5	D6	D7	D8	D9	D10	D11	D12	D13	D14
FELLOW	D1	D2	D3	D4	D5	D6	D7	D8	D9	D10	D11	D12	D13	D14

How was week Three? – Journal Entry	How was week Four? – Journal Entry

Days I prayed, read my bible, worked on my craft and fellowshipped.

PRAYED	D1	D2	D3	D4	D5	D6	D7	D8	D9	D10	D11	D12	D13	D14
READ	D1	D2	D3	D4	D5	D6	D7	D8	D9	D10	D11	D12	D13	D14
CRAFT	D1	D2	D3	D4	D5	D6	D7	D8	D9	D10	D11	D12	D13	D14
FELLOW	D1	D2	D3	D4	D5	D6	D7	D8	D9	D10	D11	D12	D13	D14

Monthly Prep 4

Highlight or circle the current month

JAN	FEB	MAR	APR	MAY	JUN	JUL	AUG	SEPT	OCT	NOV	DEC

Personal Goals and desired outcomes for this month

Verse Marinade for the month (Memorize) →	1 Timothy 6:6-8
Bible Reading for the month →	The Book of John

Monthly Progress 4

How do you view your singleness at this moment?	Not good	Ok	Great

Why these feelings?

What good, bad or ugly things showed up in your heart this month?

Good	Bad	Ugly

What do you need to do to improve in each area?

Levelled up: Did you level up or leveled down this month:

In Contentment	Levelled Up	Levelled Down	# 1-10
In your Relationship w/ God			
With your Vices or Struggles			
On working on your craft			
With your family			
With the fruits of the spirit			
Any prospects this month? If So who? →			
Did you accomplish your goals this month?		Yes	No
Did you receive the desired outcomes for this month		Yes	No

If no what interfered?	If yes what helped?

How was week One? – Journal Entry	How was week Two? – Journal Entry

Days I prayed, read my bible, worked on my craft and fellowshipped. (Circle)

PRAYED	D1	D2	D3	D4	D5	D6	D7	D8	D9	D10	D11	D12	D13	D14
READ	D1	D2	D3	D4	D5	D6	D7	D8	D9	D10	D11	D12	D13	D14
CRAFT	D1	D2	D3	D4	D5	D6	D7	D8	D9	D10	D11	D12	D13	D14
FELLOW	D1	D2	D3	D4	D5	D6	D7	D8	D9	D10	D11	D12	D13	D14

How was week Three? – Journal Entry	How was week Four? – Journal Entry

Days I prayed, read my bible, worked on my craft and fellowshipped.

PRAYED	D1	D2	D3	D4	D5	D6	D7	D8	D9	D10	D11	D12	D13	D14
READ	D1	D2	D3	D4	D5	D6	D7	D8	D9	D10	D11	D12	D13	D14
CRAFT	D1	D2	D3	D4	D5	D6	D7	D8	D9	D10	D11	D12	D13	D14
FELLOW	D1	D2	D3	D4	D5	D6	D7	D8	D9	D10	D11	D12	D13	D14

Monthly Prep 5											
Highlight or circle the current month											
JAN	FEB	MAR	APR	MAY	JUN	JUL	AUG	SEPT	OCT	NOV	DEC

Personal Goals and desired outcomes for this month

Verse Marinade for the month (Memorize) →	1 Peter 3:15
Bible Reading for the month →	The Book of Acts

Monthly Progress 5

How do you view your singleness at this moment?	Not good	Ok	Great

Why these feelings?

What good, bad or ugly things showed up in your heart this month?		
Good	Bad	Ugly

What do you need to do to improve in each area?

Levelled up: Did you level up or leveled down this month:			
In Contentment	Levelled Up	Levelled Down	# 1-10
In your Relationship w/ God			
With your Vices or Struggles			
On working on your craft			
With your family			
With the fruits of the spirit			

Any prospects this month? If So who? →			
Did you accomplish your goals this month?		Yes	No
Did you receive the desired outcomes for this month		Yes	No

If no what interfered?	If yes what helped?

How was week One? – Journal Entry	How was week Two? – Journal Entry

Days I prayed, read my bible, worked on my craft and fellowshipped. (Circle)

PRAYED	D1	D2	D3	D4	D5	D6	D7	D8	D9	D10	D11	D12	D13	D14
READ	D1	D2	D3	D4	D5	D6	D7	D8	D9	D10	D11	D12	D13	D14
CRAFT	D1	D2	D3	D4	D5	D6	D7	D8	D9	D10	D11	D12	D13	D14
FELLOW	D1	D2	D3	D4	D5	D6	D7	D8	D9	D10	D11	D12	D13	D14

How was week Three? – Journal Entry	How was week Four? – Journal Entry

Days I prayed, read my bible, worked on my craft and fellowshipped.

PRAYED	D1	D2	D3	D4	D5	D6	D7	D8	D9	D10	D11	D12	D13	D14
READ	D1	D2	D3	D4	D5	D6	D7	D8	D9	D10	D11	D12	D13	D14
CRAFT	D1	D2	D3	D4	D5	D6	D7	D8	D9	D10	D11	D12	D13	D14
FELLOW	D1	D2	D3	D4	D5	D6	D7	D8	D9	D10	D11	D12	D13	D14

Monthly Prep 6											
Highlight or circle the current month											
JAN	FEB	MAR	APR	MAY	JUN	JUL	AUG	SEPT	OCT	NOV	DEC

Personal Goals and desired outcomes for this month

Verse Marinade for the month (Memorize) →	Colossians 3:23
Bible Reading for the month →	The Book of Matthew

Monthly Progress 6

How do you view your singleness at this moment?	Not good	Ok	Great

Why these feelings?

What good, bad or ugly things showed up in your heart this month?

Good	Bad	Ugly

What do you need to do to improve in each area?

Levelled up: Did you level up or leveled down this month:

	Levelled Up	Levelled Down	# 1-10
In Contentment			
In your Relationship w/ God			
With your Vices or Struggles			
On working on your craft			
With your family			
With the fruits of the spirit			
Any prospects this month? If So who? →			
Did you accomplish your goals this month?		Yes	No
Did you receive the desired outcomes for this month		Yes	No

If no what interfered?	If yes what helped?

How was week One? – Journal Entry	How was week Two? – Journal Entry

Days I prayed, read my bible, worked on my craft and fellowshipped. (Circle)

PRAYED	D1	D2	D3	D4	D5	D6	D7	D8	D9	D10	D11	D12	D13	D14
READ	D1	D2	D3	D4	D5	D6	D7	D8	D9	D10	D11	D12	D13	D14
CRAFT	D1	D2	D3	D4	D5	D6	D7	D8	D9	D10	D11	D12	D13	D14
FELLOW	D1	D2	D3	D4	D5	D6	D7	D8	D9	D10	D11	D12	D13	D14

How was week Three? – Journal Entry	How was week Four? – Journal Entry

Days I prayed, read my bible, worked on my craft and fellowshipped.

PRAYED	D1	D2	D3	D4	D5	D6	D7	D8	D9	D10	D11	D12	D13	D14
READ	D1	D2	D3	D4	D5	D6	D7	D8	D9	D10	D11	D12	D13	D14
CRAFT	D1	D2	D3	D4	D5	D6	D7	D8	D9	D10	D11	D12	D13	D14
FELLOW	D1	D2	D3	D4	D5	D6	D7	D8	D9	D10	D11	D12	D13	D14

Monthly Prep 7											
Highlight or circle the current month											
JAN	FEB	MAR	APR	MAY	JUN	JUL	AUG	SEPT	OCT	NOV	DEC
Personal Goals and desired outcomes for this month											

Verse Marinade for the month (Memorize) →	Matthew 6:33
Bible Reading for the month →	The Book of Mark

Monthly Progress 7			
How do you view your singleness at this moment?	Not good	Ok	Great
Why these feelings?			

What good, bad or ugly things showed up in your heart this month?

Good	Bad	Ugly

What do you need to do to improve in each area?

Levelled up: Did you level up or leveled down this month:			
In Contentment	Levelled Up	Levelled Down	# 1-10
In your Relationship w/ God			
With your Vices or Struggles			
On working on your craft			
With your family			
With the fruits of the spirit			
Any prospects this month? If So who? →			
Did you accomplish your goals this month?		Yes	No
Did you receive the desired outcomes for this month		Yes	No

If no what interfered?	If yes what helped?

How was week One? – Journal Entry	How was week Two? – Journal Entry

Days I prayed, read my bible, worked on my craft and fellowshipped. (Circle)

PRAYED	D1	D2	D3	D4	D5	D6	D7	D8	D9	D10	D11	D12	D13	D14
READ	D1	D2	D3	D4	D5	D6	D7	D8	D9	D10	D11	D12	D13	D14
CRAFT	D1	D2	D3	D4	D5	D6	D7	D8	D9	D10	D11	D12	D13	D14
FELLOW	D1	D2	D3	D4	D5	D6	D7	D8	D9	D10	D11	D12	D13	D14

How was week Three? – Journal Entry	How was week Four? – Journal Entry

Days I prayed, read my bible, worked on my craft and fellowshipped.

PRAYED	D1	D2	D3	D4	D5	D6	D7	D8	D9	D10	D11	D12	D13	D14
READ	D1	D2	D3	D4	D5	D6	D7	D8	D9	D10	D11	D12	D13	D14
CRAFT	D1	D2	D3	D4	D5	D6	D7	D8	D9	D10	D11	D12	D13	D14
FELLOW	D1	D2	D3	D4	D5	D6	D7	D8	D9	D10	D11	D12	D13	D14

Monthly Prep 8											
Highlight or circle the current month											
JAN	FEB	MAR	APR	MAY	JUN	JUL	AUG	SEPT	OCT	NOV	DEC

Personal Goals and desired outcomes for this month

Verse Marinade for the month (Memorize) →	Proverbs 16:3
Bible Reading for the month →	The Book of Luke

Monthly Progress 8

How do you view your singleness at this moment?	Not good	Ok	Great

Why these feelings?

What good, bad or ugly things showed up in your heart this month?

Good	Bad	Ugly

What do you need to do to improve in each area?

Levelled up: Did you level up or leveled down this month:

In Contentment	Levelled Up	Levelled Down	# 1-10
In your Relationship w/ God			
With your Vices or Struggles			
On working on your craft			
With your family			
With the fruits of the spirit			
Any prospects this month? If So who? →			
Did you accomplish your goals this month?		Yes	No
Did you receive the desired outcomes for this month		Yes	No

If no what interfered?	If yes what helped?

How was week One? – Journal Entry	How was week Two? – Journal Entry

Days I prayed, read my bible, worked on my craft and fellowshipped. (Circle)

PRAYED	D1	D2	D3	D4	D5	D6	D7	D8	D9	D10	D11	D12	D13	D14
READ	D1	D2	D3	D4	D5	D6	D7	D8	D9	D10	D11	D12	D13	D14
CRAFT	D1	D2	D3	D4	D5	D6	D7	D8	D9	D10	D11	D12	D13	D14
FELLOW	D1	D2	D3	D4	D5	D6	D7	D8	D9	D10	D11	D12	D13	D14

How was week Three? – Journal Entry	How was week Four? – Journal Entry

Days I prayed, read my bible, worked on my craft and fellowshipped.

PRAYED	D1	D2	D3	D4	D5	D6	D7	D8	D9	D10	D11	D12	D13	D14
READ	D1	D2	D3	D4	D5	D6	D7	D8	D9	D10	D11	D12	D13	D14
CRAFT	D1	D2	D3	D4	D5	D6	D7	D8	D9	D10	D11	D12	D13	D14
FELLOW	D1	D2	D3	D4	D5	D6	D7	D8	D9	D10	D11	D12	D13	D14

Monthly Prep 9											
Highlight or circle the current month											
JAN	FEB	MAR	APR	MAY	JUN	JUL	AUG	SEPT	OCT	NOV	DEC

Personal Goals and desired outcomes for this month

Verse Marinade for the month (Memorize) →	Luke 12:15
Bible Reading for the month →	The Book of John

Monthly Progress 9			
How do you view your singleness at this moment?	Not good	Ok	Great

Why these feelings?

What good, bad or ugly things showed up in your heart this month?		
Good	Bad	Ugly

What do you need to do to improve in each area?

Levelled up: Did you level up or leveled down this month:			
In Contentment	Levelled Up	Levelled Down	# 1-10
In your Relationship w/ God			
With your Vices or Struggles			
On working on your craft			
With your family			
With the fruits of the spirit			
Any prospects this month? If So who? →			
Did you accomplish your goals this month?		Yes	No
Did you receive the desired outcomes for this month		Yes	No

If no what interfered?	If yes what helped?

How was week One? – Journal Entry	How was week Two? – Journal Entry

Days I prayed, read my bible, worked on my craft and fellowshipped. (Circle)

PRAYED	D1	D2	D3	D4	D5	D6	D7	D8	D9	D10	D11	D12	D13	D14
READ	D1	D2	D3	D4	D5	D6	D7	D8	D9	D10	D11	D12	D13	D14
CRAFT	D1	D2	D3	D4	D5	D6	D7	D8	D9	D10	D11	D12	D13	D14
FELLOW	D1	D2	D3	D4	D5	D6	D7	D8	D9	D10	D11	D12	D13	D14

How was week Three? – Journal Entry	How was week Four? – Journal Entry

Days I prayed, read my bible, worked on my craft and fellowshipped.

PRAYED	D1	D2	D3	D4	D5	D6	D7	D8	D9	D10	D11	D12	D13	D14
READ	D1	D2	D3	D4	D5	D6	D7	D8	D9	D10	D11	D12	D13	D14
CRAFT	D1	D2	D3	D4	D5	D6	D7	D8	D9	D10	D11	D12	D13	D14
FELLOW	D1	D2	D3	D4	D5	D6	D7	D8	D9	D10	D11	D12	D13	D14

Monthly Prep 10											
Highlight or circle the current month											
JAN	FEB	MAR	APR	MAY	JUN	JUL	AUG	SEPT	OCT	NOV	DEC
Personal Goals and desired outcomes for this month											

Verse Marinade for the month (Memorize) →	2 Corinthians 12:10
Bible Reading for the month →	The Book of Acts

Monthly Progress 10			
How do you view your singleness at this moment?	Not good	Ok	Great
Why these feelings?			

What good, bad or ugly things showed up in your heart this month?

Good	Bad	Ugly

What do you need to do to improve in each area?

Levelled up: Did you level up or leveled down this month:			
In Contentment	Levelled Up	Levelled Down	# 1-10
In your Relationship w/ God			
With your Vices or Struggles			
On working on your craft			
With your family			
With the fruits of the spirit			
Any prospects this month? If So who? →			
Did you accomplish your goals this month?			Yes / No
Did you receive the desired outcomes for this month			Yes / No

If no what interfered?	If yes what helped?

How was week One? – Journal Entry	How was week Two? – Journal Entry

Days I prayed, read my bible, worked on my craft and fellowshipped. (Circle)

PRAYED	D1	D2	D3	D4	D5	D6	D7	D8	D9	D10	D11	D12	D13	D14
READ	D1	D2	D3	D4	D5	D6	D7	D8	D9	D10	D11	D12	D13	D14
CRAFT	D1	D2	D3	D4	D5	D6	D7	D8	D9	D10	D11	D12	D13	D14
FELLOW	D1	D2	D3	D4	D5	D6	D7	D8	D9	D10	D11	D12	D13	D14

How was week Three? – Journal Entry	How was week Four? – Journal Entry

Days I prayed, read my bible, worked on my craft and fellowshipped.

PRAYED	D1	D2	D3	D4	D5	D6	D7	D8	D9	D10	D11	D12	D13	D14
READ	D1	D2	D3	D4	D5	D6	D7	D8	D9	D10	D11	D12	D13	D14
CRAFT	D1	D2	D3	D4	D5	D6	D7	D8	D9	D10	D11	D12	D13	D14
FELLOW	D1	D2	D3	D4	D5	D6	D7	D8	D9	D10	D11	D12	D13	D14

Monthly Prep 11	
Highlight or circle the current month	
JAN | FEB | MAR | APR | MAY | JUN | JUL | AUG | SEPT | OCT | NOV | DEC	
Personal Goals and desired outcomes for this month	
Verse Marinade for the month (Memorize) →	Isaiah 26:3
Bible Reading for the month →	The Book of Ephesians

Monthly Progress 11			
How do you view your singleness at this moment?	Not good	Ok	Great
Why these feelings?			

What good, bad or ugly things showed up in your heart this month?		
Good	Bad	Ugly

What do you need to do to improve in each area?

Levelled up: Did you level up or leveled down this month:			
In Contentment	Levelled Up	Levelled Down	# 1-10
In your Relationship w/ God			
With your Vices or Struggles			
On working on your craft			
With your family			
With the fruits of the spirit			
Any prospects this month? If So who? →			
Did you accomplish your goals this month?		Yes	No
Did you receive the desired outcomes for this month		Yes	No
If no what interfered?	If yes what helped?		

How was week One? – Journal Entry	How was week Two? – Journal Entry

Days I prayed, read my bible, worked on my craft and fellowshipped. (Circle)

PRAYED	D1	D2	D3	D4	D5	D6	D7	D8	D9	D10	D11	D12	D13	D14
READ	D1	D2	D3	D4	D5	D6	D7	D8	D9	D10	D11	D12	D13	D14
CRAFT	D1	D2	D3	D4	D5	D6	D7	D8	D9	D10	D11	D12	D13	D14
FELLOW	D1	D2	D3	D4	D5	D6	D7	D8	D9	D10	D11	D12	D13	D14

How was week Three? – Journal Entry	How was week Four? – Journal Entry

Days I prayed, read my bible, worked on my craft and fellowshipped.

PRAYED	D1	D2	D3	D4	D5	D6	D7	D8	D9	D10	D11	D12	D13	D14
READ	D1	D2	D3	D4	D5	D6	D7	D8	D9	D10	D11	D12	D13	D14
CRAFT	D1	D2	D3	D4	D5	D6	D7	D8	D9	D10	D11	D12	D13	D14
FELLOW	D1	D2	D3	D4	D5	D6	D7	D8	D9	D10	D11	D12	D13	D14

Monthly Prep 12	
Highlight or circle the current month	
JAN | FEB | MAR | APR | MAY | JUN | JUL | AUG | SEPT | OCT | NOV | DEC	
Personal Goals and desired outcomes for this month	
Verse Marinade for the month (Memorize) →	Philippians 4:19
Bible Reading for the month →	The Book of Romans

Monthly Progress 12		
How do you view your singleness at this moment?		Not good | Ok | Great
Why these feelings?		
What good, bad or ugly things showed up in your heart this month?		
Good	Bad	Ugly
What do you need to do to improve in each area?		

Levelled up: Did you level up or leveled down this month:			
In Contentment	Levelled Up	Levelled Down	# 1-10
In your Relationship w/ God			
With your Vices or Struggles			
On working on your craft			
With your family			
With the fruits of the spirit			
Any prospects this month? If So who? →			
Did you accomplish your goals this month?		Yes	No
Did you receive the desired outcomes for this month		Yes	No
If no what interfered?	If yes what helped?		

How was week One? – Journal Entry	How was week Two? – Journal Entry

Days I prayed, read my bible, worked on my craft and fellowshipped. (Circle)

PRAYED	D1	D2	D3	D4	D5	D6	D7	D8	D9	D10	D11	D12	D13	D14
READ	D1	D2	D3	D4	D5	D6	D7	D8	D9	D10	D11	D12	D13	D14
CRAFT	D1	D2	D3	D4	D5	D6	D7	D8	D9	D10	D11	D12	D13	D14
FELLOW	D1	D2	D3	D4	D5	D6	D7	D8	D9	D10	D11	D12	D13	D14

How was week Three? – Journal Entry	How was week Four? – Journal Entry

Days I prayed, read my bible, worked on my craft and fellowshipped.

PRAYED	D1	D2	D3	D4	D5	D6	D7	D8	D9	D10	D11	D12	D13	D14
READ	D1	D2	D3	D4	D5	D6	D7	D8	D9	D10	D11	D12	D13	D14
CRAFT	D1	D2	D3	D4	D5	D6	D7	D8	D9	D10	D11	D12	D13	D14
FELLOW	D1	D2	D3	D4	D5	D6	D7	D8	D9	D10	D11	D12	D13	D14

Wins and Lessons (How to handle a BREAK UP)

Take some time below to write down all of the wins and the lessons you received from this relationship. Remember losing and learning all boils down to perspective. After you have answered the questions below make sure to read through what to do during a break up.

Persons Name:			
How long did the relationship last?	Years:		Months:
What happened to cause the break up			

Who's fault?	Yours	Theirs	
Who broke up with who?	I did	They did	
Have you forgiven them?	Yes	No	
Have you forgiven yourself?	Yes	No	
How severe was the break up?	Severe	Not severe	
How strong is your tie or hold to them?	Strong	Mild	Weak
How sexual was the relationship?	Extremely	Somewhat	Not at all
What do you need to do to heal from this relationship			

How's your relationship with God?

What were the wins	What were the lessons

How to handle a B.R.E.A.K. U.P.
1. Number one **Breathe** you are alive! Never forget; it could have been worse. Take some time to breathe and relax and really think through all the red flags or the reasons you may have caused the relationship to end.
2. Secondly, **Reach** out to God and to your proven accountability. Sometimes we get lost in our relationships and forget about God and our accountability. This is the perfect time to reach out to both parties and let God the Doctor and your accountability the nurses help you heal.
3. Thirdly, **Empty** yourself of all bitterness, resentment and unforgiveness. These 3 things are natural emotions that sometimes birth out of break ups. Take some time to vent and empty yourself out of all negative feelings about the person, the situation or even with God. And remember the best way to forgive is to remember what you was forgiven of.
4. Fourthly, **Avoid** isolation. You cannot win this battle alone you need your village. Who are those people who don't mind being patient with you as you heal? If you don't have any close friends where could you go serve often to be around people?
5. Number five, **Kindly** live your life. Don't seek revenge just seek to be kind. Sink yourself in the presence of God constantly so that you will always be full of joy. You don't have to prove anything just show up to the party where God has prepared a table for you in the presence of your enemies *clears throat* your ex! Lol jk!
6. Number six, **Untie** and **Uproot**. What kind of tie did you have with this person? Was it strong, mild or weak? In order to heal you have to heal deeply and you have to make sure you untie any soul-ties and uproot any strongholds. I talk more about soul-ties and strongholds in my book The Purpose of Freedom. You can get it today on Amazon.
7. Lastly, **Push** through. It is not going to be easy but I promise you will look back at all of this and say I'm so glad that it happen. The older you get and the closer you get to God the more you will begin to see why things happened the way that they did. Let them go and Let God do what he does best and that's heal and hook you up. Trust the process you 76er!

Winning and Learning. (Leveling Up – Engaged and Married)

Take some time below to write down all of the wins and the lessons you are learning as you grow in love with your significant other. Answer the questions below and read through the things you need to consider while leveling up!

Persons name:			
What or who brought you guys together?			
How long have you guys been in a relationship so for?	Years:	Months:	
What level have you guys leveled up to	Engagement	Marriage	#_____ years married
What have you learned about yourself from the last level or year?	What have you learned about your significant other from the last level or year		
How much of God is in your relationship now and why is it important to have him in your relationship.			
Where do you see guys this time next year? What must you do to make this a reality?			
In what ways are you guys winning together	In what ways are you guys learning together?		

What to consider when it's time to L.E.V.E.L. U.P.

1. Number one, **Let** Go! This point has a double meaning. In order to be present in your relationship today and tomorrow you have to let go of all the negative things, experiences and the ex's of your past. You also must let go and let God. You must let go of all of your carnal ways or habits and let God lead you in your relationship. So many people want control in their relationship but they're unable to handle the seas of life. Let God be the captain of your relation-ship!
2. Secondly, **Embrace** your individuality and the individuality of your significant other. A relationship is comprised of two individuals meaning two unique people who both have something great to provide the relationship. You and your significant other have within yourselves cargo full of valuables. Let each other be great and contribute (you)niquely to the relationship and don't rob them of themselves. Let them be godly great.
3. Thirdly, always be **Vocal**. A lot of relationships have ended due to poor communication. So many people either hold on to things that need to be said or say what needs to be said but just in the wrong tone. Communication is important in every relationship because without it there will be chaos. Always aim to talk things out and to talk up your significant other. Never forget that your significant words have significant weight to your significant other. Be intentional in using your words and tailor them to how your significant other likes to receive them.
4. Fourthly, continue to **Educate** yourself. Every person that is in Christ is a new creature; their old things are passing away and every day they are becoming new. The person you are with if they are in Christ are going to evolve and you have to continue to study them to ensure you can serve their new self. Stay close to your significant other; read their body language, listen to what they say when they go down rabbit holes, take the time to see what catches their eye and once you have seen and heard what they had to say; take what you've heard and make plans to serve them and their aspiration. There is nothing better than feeling understood. It's not easy evolving in God and its hard sometimes to communicate it. Every day aim to know them more.
5. Fifthly, **Love** without expectations. Selfless love is the best kind of love. Don't let selfishness or unrealistic expectations suffocate your relationship. Let them breathe and enjoy the God infused climate of your relationship.

6. Number six, stay **Under** God. Any relationship not under God is vulnerable. Keep God first and in the center of every aspect of your relationship. He is the only one that can sustain your relationship. Don't allow anything to drift your relationships focus off of God.
7. Lastly, know your **Place**. What's your part in the relationship? What are your responsibilities? Take some time to establish each other's role and make sure you both stay consistent in your roles because you guys are a team and when one player is off it can affect the entire team. Define your roles and shine in your roles and let God be glorified through it.

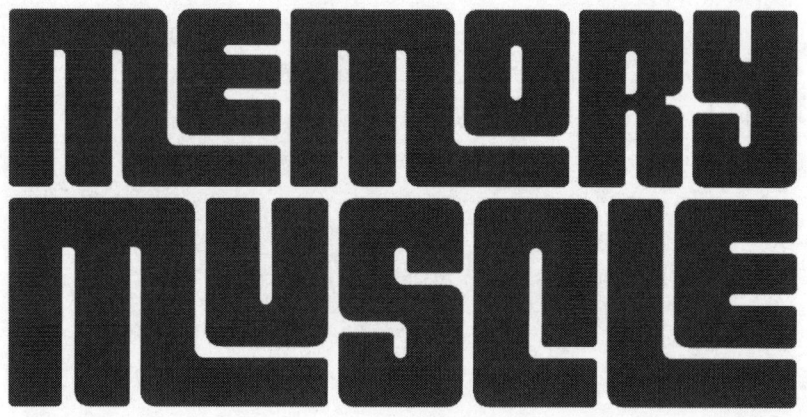

↑
GAMES AVAILABLE NOW AT MYCOACHJOSH.COM

Made in the USA
San Bernardino, CA
28 December 2018